The Complete Mediterranean Diet Cookbook

Quick and Delicious Recipes
for Everyday Enjoyment
incl. 21-Day Meal Plan

Thomas Hughes

Copyright © [2021] [Thomas Hughes]

All rights reserved

All rights for this book here presented belong exclusively to the author. Usage or reproduction of the text is forbidden and requires a clear consent of the author in case of expectations.

ISBN - 9798774336685

TABLE OF CONTENTS

Introduction 7
  What Is The Mediterranean Diet? 7
  What To Eat & Not To Eat Whilst On The Mediterranean Diet 8
  Breakfast 11
    Market Vegetable Quiche 11
    Scrambled Eggs with Tomato, Spinach and Ricotta 12
    Loaded Veggie Bake 13
    Quinoa and Feta Egg Muffins 14
    Overnight Oatmeal with Fruit and Yogurt 15
    Muesli with Apples and Raisins 16
    Blueberry Yogurt Parfait 17
    Grab 'N Go Fruit Smoothies 18
    Green Smoothies 18
    Baba Ghanouj 19
    Shakshuka 20

  Salads 21
    Classic Greek Salad 21
    Spinach, Tomato and Mushroom Salad 22
    Tuscan-Style Salad with Green Olives and Roasted Peppers 23
    Sugar Snap Pea and Radish Salad 24
    Moroccan Carrot Salad 25
    Watermelon Feta and Mint Salad 26
    Blood Orange Salad with Lemon Vinaigrette 27
    Panzanella with Cucumbers and Cherry Tomatoes 28
    Kale with Pine Nuts and Raisins 29
    Brussels Sprouts and Chickpea Salad 30
    Fattoush 31

  Sides & Snacks 32
    Braised Green Beans with Mint and Feta 32
    Porcini Mushroom Risotto with Peas 33
    Sweet and Savory Basmati Rice Salad 34
    Simple Lebanese Rice 35

Tabbouleh 36
Cauliflower Couscous 37
Lebanese Potatoes 38
Roasted Vegetables with Garlic and Thyme 39
Feta Dill Dip 40
Fruit, Nut and Seed Bars 41
Easy Creamy Hummus 42

Meat 43
Mediterranean Stuffed Chicken 43
Chicken, Peppers and Red Onion Kebabs 44
Braised Chicken Breasts with Bulgur Pilaf 45
Herb Roasted Lamb Chops 46
Braised Lamb Shanks 47
Sirloin Ribbons 49
Roasted Garlic Dijon Pork Loin 50
Pork Chops with Vegetable Medley 51
Paella Valenciana 52

Fish & Seafood 53
Lemon Garlic Baked Cod 53
Herb Roasted Sea Bass 54
Baked Snapper with Tomatoes and Olives 55
Lemon-Herb Salmon with Sicilian Caponata 56
Baked Lump Crab Cakes 57
Baked Tuna Steaks with Garlic Aioli 58

Pasta 59
Hearty Lasagna with Lentils and Zucchini 59
Whole Grain Lasagna with Eggplant and Olives 61
Pasta Primavera 62
Tuscan Baked Ziti 63

Vegetarian 64
Moroccan Root Vegetable Tagine 64
Turkish Stuffed Eggplant 65
Greek Hand Pies 67
Chickpea, Zucchini and Tomatoes with Pesto 68
Garlic and Herb Lentil Salad 69

Desserts 70
Berries and Honey Ginger Yogurt 70
Yogurt Panna Cotta with Honey 71

Dates with Yogurt, Citrus and Honey 72
Strawberry Granita 73
Strawberry Topped Almond Cake 74
Apple Granola and Yogurt Mini Trifle 75
Jeweled Fruit en Papillote 76
Fruit Cup Chia Pudding 77
Dried Figs with Ricotta and Walnuts 78
Cherry Clafoutis 79
Turkish Yogurt Cake 80

BONUS: 21 Day Mediterranean Diet Weight Loss Plan 81
Day 1 81
Day 2 82
Day 3 84
Day 4 85
Day 5 86
Day 6 87
Day 7 88
Day 8 89
Day 9 90
Day 10 92
Day 11 94
Day 12 95
Day 13 96
Day 14 97
Day 15 98
Day 16 100
Day 17 101
Day 18 102
Day 19 104
Day 20 105
Day 21 106

Disclaimer 108

Introduction

What Is The Mediterranean Diet?

The Mediterranean Diet is a traditional way of eating which has been practiced in Mediterranean regions for thousands of years. It's a diet based on a wide variety of fresh, whole foods that keep blood sugar and cholesterol levels in check. Today, many nutritionists recommend that people follow a Mediterranean diet to lose weight and improve their health.

The Mediterranean Diet is based on the pre-industrial lifestyle followed by the people in the Mediterranean region, including Greece, Italy, Portugal and Spain, and neighbouring countries. With globalization came a rise in refined and fast food for convenience which led to a shift in diet away from wholesome food sources rich in vitamins and minerals to a diet filled with processed fats and high amounts of sugar. This dietary change has led to many suffering from various health ailments and obesity. Many people are switching to a Mediterranean diet and are enjoying better health and quality of life.

The Mediterranean Diet is an eating plan that focuses on fresh, whole foods. It is a traditional diet that emphasizes the intake of vegetables, fruits, whole grains, beans, nuts, legumes, and olive oil. It also allows for meals with fish, poultry, and moderate amounts of red meat. It is low in fat and high in fiber and ensures a good source of vitamins, minerals, and antioxidants. The goal of the Mediterranean Diet is to eat more whole foods that are fresh or minimally processed. This dietary pattern is best known as a healthy eating option that helps keep blood sugar and cholesterol levels under control, which makes it a healthy weight loss diet.

The success of the Mediterranean Diet is due to its ease, as many meals can be prepared within 30 mins and high content of whole foods and healthy fats which keep you feeling fuller for longer. In this book, you will find many Mediterranean-inspired recipes to choose from that are easy to make and can be enjoyed with family and friends. As a bonus, you will also find a 21-day meal plan to get you started with your weight loss journey for the long term.

People are starting to realize that the Mediterranean Diet is not just about good food, but it's about better health. Eating real food with little to no added sugar or processed food along with regular exercise and maintaining good relationships is key to a happy and healthier life.

Benefits of the Mediterranean Diet
- Weight loss
- Lowers cholesterol
- Lowers blood pressure
- Reduces risk of heart disease
- Reduces risk of a stroke
- Prevents or manage Type 2 diabetes
- Protects against some cancers
- Encourages exercise and a balanced healthy lifestyle

What To Eat & Not To Eat Whilst On The Mediterranean Diet

The Mediterranean diet does not involve fasting or restrictive eating. You can enjoy many of your favourite meals by switching to whole foods and adjusting your portions to include more plant-based foods. The Mediterranean diet helps to reduce the levels of 'poor' cholesterol and the risk of cardiovascular disease, including strokes and heart attacks. It also aims to reduce obesity. Adding spices and herbs to your dishes is a great way to add more colour and flavour as well as an added antioxidant boost.

The ancient Mediterranean diet could be the most effective diet for health and weight loss. The benefits are found in the classic, delicious staples of the Mediterranean diet. Olive oil contains healthy monounsaturated fats. Studies have found that eating olive oil instead of foods rich in

saturated fat greatly increases the amount of energy the body uses at rest, and even when sitting or sleeping, you will be burning more calories. Greek yogurt can relieve hunger, improve feelings of fullness, regulate blood sugar levels, minimize cravings, and avoid overeating, as it has substantially more protein per ounce than virtually every other ready-to-eat food. Including micronutrients - vitamins, minerals, antioxidants, and phytochemicals - is key to weight loss. The micronutrients in vegetables revive your metabolism and fuel your body with energy. To lose weight, you need to have both soluble and insoluble fiber, and no other single food has more than beans of both these types. A typical Western diet does not include enough omega-3 fatty acids that are important for metabolism, sensitivity to blood sugar, and any other factor that affects the ability of our bodies to burn fat. Decreasing how much processed food you eat whilst eating more omega-3 rich fish and seafood will help bring the right balance of fatty acids into your body.

If you are looking to lose weight, here are macros on the Mediterranean diet plan:
- 50% Carbohydrates derived from vegetables, nuts, legumes, and whole grains
- 35% Healthy oils, nuts, seeds, and fish fats
- 15% Protein from legumes, fish, nuts, milk, poultry, and eggs

It is more important that you apply the principles of the Mediterranean diet plan in a way that is realistic for your lifestyle and current level of health, rather than trying to follow a strict set of rules that you won't keep up with for long. There are a few limits to the Mediterranean diet. The focus is to develop a healthy lifestyle that you can enjoy and stick with in the long run.

Healthy Foods To Eat On The Mediterranean Diet
- Seafood & Fish: Tuna, Anchovies, Sardines, Mackerel, Herring, Salmon, Trout, Cod, Barramundi, Sea Bass, Shrimp, Crab, Oysters, Mussels, Clams
- Vegetables: Tomato, Kale, Spinach, Arugula, Collard greens, Swiss chard, Celery, Broccoli, Cauliflower, Carrots, Brussel sprouts, Cucumbers, Green Beans, Eggplant, Zucchini, Squash, Onions, Scallions, Shallots, Garlic, Bell pepper, Mushrooms, Artichokes, Cabbage, Fennel, Leeks, Asparagus, Potatoes, Sweet potatoes, Turnips, Yams, Beets
- Fruits: Apples, Pears, Bananas, Oranges, Clementine, Lemons, Limes, Grapefruit, Grapes, Dates, Figs, Cantaloupe, Melon, Peaches, Apricots, Plums, Pomegranate, Strawberries, Blueberries, Raspberries, Blackberries, Cherries, Avocados
- Nuts & Seeds: Almonds, Walnuts, Macadamia nuts, Hazelnuts, Cashews, Pistachios, Pine nuts, Sesame seeds, Sunflower seeds, Pumpkin seeds
- Legumes: Beans, Peas, Lentils, Chickpeas
- Whole-grains: Oats, Brown Rice, Barley, Bulgur, Buckwheat, Corn, Whole Grain Bread, Pita Bread, Pasta, Couscous, Quinoa
- Meat: Chicken, Duck, Turkey
- Diary: Cheese, Greek Yogurt, Eggs, Milk
- Fats: (Extra Virgin) Olive Oil, Avocado Oil

- Other: Olives, Honey, Wine

Unhealthy Foods To Avoid On The Mediterranean Diet
- No processed meats
- Avoid Sugar, use natural sweeteners
- White Rice
- Butter, use olive oil
- Sesame oil
- Pam oil
- Limit consumption of beef, pork, or lamb
- Hard liquor
- Ice cream
- Red wine - limit to one or two glasses a day

Breakfast

MARKET VEGETABLE QUICHE

Time: 1 hr 25 mins | Serves 6
Net carbs: 6g | Fat: 16g
Protein: 16g | Kcal: 230

INGREDIENTS

- 2 tbsp virgin olive oil
- 1 large onion, cut in half lengthwise and sliced into half circles
- Salt
- 600 g / 21 oz lightly packed spinach
- 1 yellow squash or zucchini, sliced
- 1 tomato, seeded and chopped
- 1 tbsp fresh rosemary leaves
- 8 large eggs
- 285 ml / 8 ⅔ oz milk
- 113 g / 4 oz grated cheddar
- Freshly ground black pepper

INSTRUCTIONS

1. Preheat the oven to 205°C / 400°F.
2. In a large skillet over medium heat, add 1 tbsp oil and heat until shimmering. Add the onion, season with salt and cook, stirring occasionally, 10 to 15 minutes or until onion is softened and lightly browned. Arrange onions over the bottom of a deep-dish glass pie pan. Set aside.
3. Add remaining oil to the skillet and heat until shimmering. Add the spinach, squash and tomatoes; cook, stirring occasionally, 3 to 5 minutes or until spinach is wilted and vegetables are softened. Stir in rosemary. Transfer vegetables to a pie pan and arrange evenly on top of onions.
4. In a medium bowl, gently beat eggs. Mix in the milk, cheese and 1 tsp salt and 1/2 tsp pepper. Pour the mixture over the vegetables.
5. Bake for 45 minutes or until the surface is slightly brown and a knife inserted in the center comes out clean.
6. Let quiche stand for 20 minutes to cool. To serve, slice into wedges.

SCRAMBLED EGGS WITH TOMATO, SPINACH AND RICOTTA

Time: 5 mins | Serves 2
Net carbs: 4g | Fat: 15g
Protein: 14g | Kcal: 209

INGREDIENTS

- 1 tbsp virgin olive oil
- 1 Roma tomato, seeded and diced
- 30 g / 1 oz lightly packed baby spinach
- 3 eggs
- 1 egg white
- Salt
- 2 tbsp ricotta cheese
- Freshly ground black pepper

INSTRUCTIONS

1. In a small bowl, add the eggs, egg white and a pinch of salt. Using a fork, gently beat the eggs.
2. In a medium skillet over medium heat, add the oil and heat until shimmering. Add the tomatoes and spinach; cook, stirring often, for 3 minutes or until the spinach is wilted.
3. Add the eggs to the spinach mixture and cook, gently folding, for 30 seconds and then add the ricotta. Continue cooking and folding the egg mixture, until egg whites are opaque.
4. Transfer serving plates. Season to taste with salt and pepper.

LOADED VEGGIE BAKE

Time: 1 hr 10 mins | Serves 8
Net carbs: 20g | Fat: 11
Protein: 22g | Kcal: 263

INGREDIENTS

- 2 tbsp virgin olive oil
- 2 cloves garlic, minced
- 100 g / 3 ½ oz sliced button mushrooms
- 220 g / 7 ¾ oz shredded carrots
- 150 g / 5 ½ oz diced bell pepper and onion mix
- 280 g / 2.8 oz firmly packed baby kale, torn into bite-size pieces
- 280 g / 10 oz frozen diced potatoes
- 470 g / 16 ½ oz fat-free shredded cheddar cheese
- 12 large eggs
- 480 ml / 17 oz semi-skimmed milk
- Salt
- Freshly ground black pepper
- 1 tsp fresh thyme leaves

INSTRUCTIONS

1. Preheat the oven to 190°C / 375°F.
2. Grease a baking dish with 1 tbsp oil. Set aside.
3. In a large skillet over medium heat, add oil and heat until shimmering. Add the mushrooms, carrots and bell pepper mix; cook, stirring occasionally, for about 5 to 7 minutes or until tender. Add the kale and cook, tossing often, 5 minutes or until softened and liquids are evaporated. Stir in potatoes. Transfer to the prepared baking dish and spread evenly on the bottom of the dish. Sprinkle vegetables with cheese.
4. In a large bowl, whisk the egg, milk, 2 tsp salt, 1/4 tsp pepper and thyme. Pour over the vegetables.
5. Bake for 40 to 50 minutes or until the top is golden brown and a knife inserted in the middle comes out clean. Let cool for 10 minutes before cutting.
6. Serve immediately or cover and refrigerate individual serving pieces for up to 5 days. Servings can also be tightly covered and frozen for up to 3 months.

QUINOA AND FETA EGG MUFFINS

Time: 40 mins | Serves 12
Net carbs: 13g | Fat: 13g
Protein: 13g | Kcal: 225

INGREDIENTS

- 4 tsp virgin olive oil
- 25 g / 1 oz finely chopped onion
- 200 g / 7 oz chopped tomatoes
- 60 g / 2 oz baby spinach (finely chopped)
- 90 g / 3 oz chopped black olives
- 1 tbsp chopped fresh oregano
- 8 eggs
- 185 g / 6 ½ oz cooked quinoa
- 150 g / 5 ⅓ oz crumbled feta cheese
- Salt
- ¼ teaspoon salt

INSTRUCTIONS

1. Preheat the oven to 175°C / 350°F.
2. Grease a muffin tin with about 2 tsp oil. Set aside.
3. In a large skillet over medium heat, add 2 tsp oil and heat until shimmering. Add the onions and cook, stirring often, 3 minutes. Add the tomatoes and the spinach and cook, tossing, 2 minutes or until vegetables are softened and spinach is wilted. Remove from heat. Stir in olives and oregano. Set aside.
4. In a large bowl, whisk eggs. Stir in quinoa, feta vegetable mixture and 1 tsp salt.
5. Pour mixture into muffin tins and bake, 30 minutes or until muffins are golden and a knife inserted into the center of a muffin comes out clean. Let them stand for 7 minutes to cool.
6. Serve immediately or cover tightly and refrigerate for up to 5 days.

OVERNIGHT OATMEAL WITH FRUIT AND YOGURT

Time: 8 hrs | Serves 1
Net carbs: 31g | Fat: 3g
Protein: 12g | Kcal: 193

INGREDIENTS

- 40 g / 1 ½ oz rolled (old-fashion) oats
- 120 ml / 4 ⅓ oz skimmed milk
- 140 g / 5 oz fat-free plain Greek yogurt
- 1 tsp chia seeds
- 95 g / 3 ⅓ oz blueberries
- 95 g / 3 ⅓ oz strawberries, cored and chopped

INSTRUCTIONS

1. In a 250ml / 8oz canning jar add oatmeal and pour in the milk. Layer yogurt, chia seeds, blueberries and strawberries.
2. Cover and refrigerate for 8 hours or overnight.
3. Serve chilled.

Note: Overnight oats can be covered tightly and refrigerated for up to 5 days.

MUESLI WITH APPLES AND RAISINS

Time: 5 mins| Serves 14
Net carbs: 40g | Fat: 17g
Protein: 11g | Kcal: 334

INGREDIENTS

- 360 g / 12 ⅔ oz rolled (old-fashion) oats
- 180 g / 6 ⅓ oz walnuts, coarsely chopped
- 130 g / 4 ½ oz sunflower seeds
- 1 tbsp virgin olive oil
- ½ tsp Salt
- ¼ tsp ground cinnamon
- 120 g / 4 ¼ oz dried apple pieces
- 80 g / 3 oz raisins

INSTRUCTIONS

1. Preheat the oven to 175°C / 350°F.
2. In a large bowl, combine the oats, walnuts, sunflower seeds, oil, salt and cinnamon. On a baking sheet, spread the mixture in a thin layer.
3. Bake for 5 minutes or until fragrant and lightly golden. Let cool. Stir in dried apples and raisins. Cover tightly and store at room temperature for up to 2 weeks.

BLUEBERRY YOGURT PARFAIT

Time: 5 mins | Serves 1
Net carbs: 35g | Fat: 2g
Protein: 20g | Kcal: 232

INGREDIENTS

- 210 g / 7 ½ oz plain fat-free Greek yogurt, divided
- 55 g / 2 oz blueberries
- 120 g / 4 ¼ oz natural granola with raisins

INSTRUCTIONS

In a serving bowl, layer half of the yogurt, the granola, the remaining yogurt and the blueberries.

GRAB 'N GO FRUIT SMOOTHIES

Time: 5 mins | Serves 1
Net carbs: 44g | Fat: 4g
Protein: 11g | Kcal: 246

INGREDIENTS

- 1 frozen banana, halved
- 190 g / 6 ¾ oz frozen blueberries
- 150 g / 5 ⅓ oz fat-free plain Greek yogurt
- 45 g / 1 ½ oz old-fashioned rolled oats
- 1 tbsp ground flax seeds
- 2 tsp lemon juice
- 1 tsp pure vanilla extract

INSTRUCTIONS

1. Add banana, blueberries, yogurt, oats, flax seeds, lemon juice, vanilla and 80 ml / 3 oz water to a blender. Cover and blend for 1 minute.
2. Add more water, if needed, and blend until your desired consistency is reached.

GREEN SMOOTHIES

Time: 5 mins | Serves 1
Net carbs: 69g | Fat: 2g
Protein: 6g | Kcal: 286

INGREDIENTS

- 20 g / ¾ oz baby kale
- 1 banana
- 100 g / 7 oz cranberries
- 125 g / 4 ½ oz blueberries
- 3 ice cubes
- 250 ml / 8 ¾ oz coconut water

INSTRUCTIONS

1. Add kale, banana, cranberries, blueberries, ice cubes, and coconut water to a blender. Cover and blend for 1 minute.
2. Add more water, if needed, and blend until your desired consistency is reached.

BABA GHANOUJ

Time: 2 hrs | Serves 2
Net carbs: 32g | Fat: 12g
Protein: 7g | Kcal: 240

INGREDIENTS

- 910 g / 2 lbs eggplant, halved lengthwise
- Salt
- Extra virgin olive oil
- 1/4 freshly squeezed lemon juice (approx.)
- 35 g / 1 ¼ oz tahini, stirred well
- 2 tbsp plain yogurt
- 2 cloves garlic, halved
- Chopped parsley leaves

INSTRUCTIONS

1. Using a sharp knife, score the flesh deeply in a cross-hatch pattern. Press on the eggplant to open the cuts and sprinkle with 1-1/2 tsp salt.
2. Set aside, cut side up, for 30 minutes.
3. Preheat the oven to 205°C / 400°F.
4. Line a baking sheet with parchment.
5. Squeeze the juice from the eggplants and discard. Using a paper towel, wipe eggplant dry. Brush cut sides completely with oil. On a parchment-lined baking sheet, arrange eggplant cut side down.
6. Bake for 1 hour or until the eggplants collapse and the flesh-side is a deep brown caramel color. Transfer eggplant to a colander over a sink and let cool for 20 minutes. Using a spoon, scoop out the flesh and let stand in the colander for 30 minutes or until room temperature. Discard stems and skin.
7. Meanwhile using a mortar and pestle, mash garlic with a generous pinch of salt into a paste. Transfer paste to a food processor.
8. Add the eggplant, lemon juice, tahini and yogurt; puree mixture.
9. Transfer to a bowl. Drizzle with olive oil. Serve garnished with parsley.

SHAKSHUKA

Time: 10 mins | Serves 6
Net carbs: 47g | Fat: 19g
Protein: 14g | Kcal: 414

INGREDIENTS

- 3 tbsp virgin olive oil
- 2 green bell peppers, cored, seeded and chopped
- 1 large yellow onion, chopped
- 2 cloves garlic, finely chopped
- 1 tsp ground coriander
- 1 tsp paprika
- 1/2 tsp ground cumin
- Pinch red pepper flakes
- Salt
- 6 tomatoes, chopped
- 110g / 4 oz tomato sauce
- 1 tsp sugar
- 6 large eggs
- 60 g / 2 oz chopped fresh parsley leaves
- 60 g / 2 oz chopped fresh mint leaves
- 6 slices thick crusty bread warmed

INSTRUCTIONS

1. In a large heavy-bottom skillet over medium heat, add the oil and heat until shimmering.
2. Add the bell pepper and onion; cook, stirring often, 5 to 7 minutes or until the vegetables are softened. Add the garlic, coriander, paprika, cumin, pepper flakes and a pinch of salt; cook, stirring, 1 minute or until the garlic is fragrant.
3. Add the tomatoes, tomato sauce and sugar; cook, stirring occasionally, 10 minutes or until the mixture starts to reduce and thicken.
4. Using the back of a spoon, make 6 indentations, spaced apart, in the tomato mixture. Carefully crack an egg into each indentation.
5. Reduce the heat to medium-low and cook, covered, until the egg whites are opaque and eggs are done to your liking. Sprinkle with parsley and mint. Season to taste with salt and
6. pepper.
7. Ladle eggs and sauce onto individual serving plates. Serve with warm crusty bread.

Salads

CLASSIC GREEK SALAD

Time: 20 mins | Serves 4
Net carbs: 23g | Fat: 24g
Protein: 18g | Kcal: 323

INGREDIENTS

- 70 ml / 2 ½ oz red wine vinegar
- 1 lemon, zest and juice
- 1 tsp dried oregano
- 1 tsp honey
- Salt
- Freshly ground black pepper
- 55 ml / 2 ½ oz extra-virgin olive oil
- 5 Persian cucumbers, halved lengthwise and cut crosswise into slices
- 12 small Roma tomatoes, cut into chunks
- 180 g / 6 ⅓ oz pitted black olives, halved
- 1 small red onion, chopped
- 115 g / 4 oz feta cheese cubes packed in brine

INSTRUCTIONS

1. In a large bowl, whisk the vinegar, lemon zest, lemon juice, oregano, honey, 1 tsp salt and ¼ tsp pepper. Slowly whisk in the olive oil until emulsified.
2. Add the cucumbers, tomatoes, olives and red onion to the vinaigrette; tossing to combine.
3. Let stand for 15 minutes to meld flavors.
4. Spoon salad onto serving plates and serve sprinkled with feta cubes.

SPINACH, TOMATO AND MUSHROOM SALAD

Time: 5 mins | Serves 2
Net carbs: 12g | Fat: 21g
Protein: 7g | Kcal: 258

INGREDIENTS

- 240 g / 8.5 oz spinach
- 150 g / 5 ¼ oz cherry tomatoes, halved
- 225 g / 8 oz cremini mushrooms, sliced
- 1/4 small red onion, sliced
- 3 tbsp virgin olive oil
- 1 tbsp lemon juice
- Salt
- Freshly ground black pepper

INSTRUCTIONS

1. Arrange spinach in 2 salad bowls. Top each with ½ of the tomatoes, mushrooms and onions.
2. In a small jar with a cover, add oil and lemon juice.
3. Season with salt and pepper. Cover the jar and shake vigorously to combine. Drizzle vinaigrette over salads.

TUSCAN-STYLE SALAD WITH GREEN OLIVES AND ROASTED PEPPERS

Time: 50 mins | Serves 6
Net carbs: 42g | Fat: 22g
Protein: 7g | Kcal: 398

INGREDIENTS

- 1 red bell pepper
- 1 yellow bell pepper
- 150 g / 1 lb Italian bread
- 140 ml / 5 ⅓ oz extra-virgin olive oil
- 285 ml / 30 oz cider vinegar
- 1 small red onion, quartered and thinly sliced
- 3 tbsp sliced green olives
- 1 tbsp minced fresh oregano leaves
- Salt
- Freshly ground black pepper

INSTRUCTIONS

1. Preheat the oven to 245°C / 475°F.
2. Line a baking sheet with foil and spray with nonstick cooking spray. Arrange peppers on their side.
3. Bake, turning once, 40 minutes or until peppers are charred, softened and slightly collapsed.
4. Transfer peppers to a paper bag and seal the bag tightly. Set aside for 15 minutes. Meanwhile, remove crusts from the bread. Discard crusts or save for another use. Cut
5. bread into cubes.
6. Transfer peppers to a cutting board. Remove the stem. Cut peppers in half and remove the seeds and ribs. Cut peppers into wide slices.
7. In a large bowl, combine roasted peppers and bread cubes. Set aside.
8. In a medium bowl, whisk together oil, vinegar, onions, olives and oregano. Season with salt and pepper. Pour dressing over bread and pepper mixture, tossing well. Let stand for 10 minutes. Serve immediately or cover tightly and set aside for up to 2 hours.

SUGAR SNAP PEA AND RADISH SALAD

Time: 15 mins | Serves 4
Net carbs: 9g | Fat: 8g
Protein: 4g | Kcal: 120

INGREDIENTS

- 340 g / 3⁄4 lb sugar snap peas trimmed, strung, cut in half diagonally
- Salt
- 5 tsp extra-virgin olive oil
- 2 tsp fresh lemon juice
- 1⁄2 tsp white wine vinegar
- 1⁄2 tsp ground sumac, divided
- 85 g / 3 oz radishes, trimmed and thinly sliced
- 55 g / 2 oz crumbled feta cheese
- Freshly ground black pepper
- 1 tbsp coarsely chopped fresh mint

INSTRUCTIONS

1. Fill a large bowl with ice water; set aside.
2. In a stockpot over medium-high heat, add 1.7 L water and 1 tsp salt; heat until boiling.
3. Add peas and cook, 2 minutes or until crisp-tender. Drain and immediately transfer to a bowl with ice water. Let cool, refreshing the cold water as needed. Transfer to a clean kitchen towel and pat dry.
4. In a small bowl, whisk oil 1-1/2 tsp lemon juice, vinegar and 1/4 tsp sumac.
5. In a large bowl, combine peas, radishes and cheese. Add dressing and toss to coat. Season with salt, pepper and remaining sumac. Drizzle with remaining lemon juice, if desired.
6. Serve garnished with mint.

MOROCCAN CARROT SALAD

Time: 5 mins | Serves 4
Net carbs: 17g | Fat: 21g
Protein: 5g | Kcal: 262

INGREDIENTS

- 2 tsp dry harissa
- 2 tbsp lemon juice
- 5 tsp extra-virgin olive oil
- Salt
- Freshly ground black
- pepper
- 340 g / 3⁄4 lb carrots, coarsely shredded
- 80 g / 3 oz raisins
- 45 g / 1 ½ oz loosely packed parsley leaves
- 50 g / 1 ¾ oz crumbled feta

INSTRUCTIONS

1. In a large bowl, whisk the harissa with the lemon juice. Gradually whisk in the oil. Season with salt and pepper.
2. Add the carrots and raisins to the dressing, tossing well to coat in the dressing.
3. Gently toss in the parsley and feta. Refrigerate until ready to serve or serve immediately.

WATERMELON FETA AND MINT SALAD

Time: 5 mins | Serves 2
Net carbs: 12g | Fat: 4g
Protein: 4g | Kcal: 96

INGREDIENTS

- 300 g / 10 ½ oz watermelon balls
- 7 g / ¼ oz crumbled feta cheese
- 2 tbsp fresh mint leaves

INSTRUCTIONS

In a shallow bowl, gently toss watermelon balls with chopped mint and crumbled feta.

BLOOD ORANGE SALAD WITH LEMON VINAIGRETTE

Time: 5 mins | Serves 2
Net carbs: 12g | Fat: 4g
Protein: 4g | Kcal: 96

INGREDIENTS

- ¼ small red onion, very thinly sliced
- 60 ml / 2 oz rice wine vinegar
- Sea salt
- Freshly ground pepper
- 4 blood oranges
- 85 g / 3 oz lightly packed arugula
- 2 tbsp extra virgin olive oil
- 2 tsp lemon juice
- 1 tbsp finely chopped mint leaves

INSTRUCTIONS

1. In a small bowl, add the red onion and vinegar, tossing well. Season with salt and pepper. Let stand for 15 minutes or until onions are softened. Drain.
2. Meanwhile, peel the oranges, removing the white pith. Using a sharp knife, thinly slice the oranges crosswise. Remove any seeds.
3. Arrange arugula on serving plates. Arrange the orange slices on the arugula. Scatter with red onions.
4. In a small jar with a cover, add the olive oil, lemon juice and mint. Cover the jar and shake vigorously until combined. Drizzle vinaigrette over the salad. Season to taste with salt and pepper.

PANZANELLA WITH CUCUMBERS AND CHERRY TOMATOES

Time: 25 mins | Serves 6
Net carbs: 53g | Fat: 26g
Protein: 11g | Kcal: 484

INGREDIENTS

- 900 g / 2 lbs tomatoes, cut into pieces
- 2 cucumbers, peeled and seeded, cut into pieces
- Salt
- 455 g / 1 lb sourdough bread, crusts removed and cut into cubes
- 190 ml / 6 ¾ oz extra-virgin olive oil, divided
- 1 shallot, minced
- 2 cloves garlic, minced
- 1/2 tsp Dijon mustard
- 2 tbsp white wine vinegar
- 10 g / ⅓ oz lightly packed basil leaves, coarsely chopped
- Freshly ground black pepper

INSTRUCTIONS

1. Preheat the oven to 190°C / 375°F.
2. Place tomatoes and cucumbers in a colander set over a bowl. Sprinkle with salt, tossing to combine. Let drain for about 15 to 30 minutes. Discard all but 70 ml of juice and set aside.
3. In a large bowl, add bread cubes and 2 tbsp oil, tossing to coat the bread. Transfer bread to a baking sheet. Bake for 15 to 20 minutes or until crisp but not browned. Let cool.
4. In the bowl with the juice, add shallot, garlic, mustard and vinegar. Whisking constantly, drizzling in the remaining oil. Season to taste with salt and pepper.
5. In a large bowl, combine tomato and cucumber mixture, bread cubes and basil. Drizzle in vinaigrette, tossing to coat. Let stand 30 minutes, tossing occasionally, until dressing is absorbed and flavors are melded.

KALE WITH PINE NUTS AND RAISINS

Time: 10 mins | Serves 6
Net carbs: 28g | Fat: 10g
Protein: 7g | Kcal: 209

INGREDIENTS

- 40 g / 1 ½ oz golden raisins
- 70 ml / 2 ½ oz hot water
- 2 tbsp pine nuts
- 3 tbsp virgin olive oil
- 1.4 kg / 3 lbs baby kale, stemmed
- 1 small red onion, thinly sliced
- 70 ml / 2 ½ oz balsamic vinegar
- 1 tsp lightly packed brown sugar
- Salt

INSTRUCTIONS

1. In a small bowl, add raisins and cover with hot water.
2. In a Dutch pot over medium heat, add the pine nuts and toast, stirring often, 5 minutes or until golden. Transfer to a plate and set aside. Increase heat to high. Add 1 tbsp oil to the
3. same Dutch pot and heat until shimmering. Add kale, in small batches and cook, stirring, until slightly softened before adding the next batch. Cook, stirring, 1 minute or until kale is evenly wilted and glossy.
4. Using tongs, transfer kale to a colander in a sink. Press down on kale to release any liquids.
5. Using paper towels, wipe out the Dutch pot and reduce heat to medium. Add remaining oil and cook until shimmering. Add the red onion and cook, stirring, 3 to 5 minutes or until softened. Drain raisins and add to shallots. Stir in vinegar and sugar; cook, stirring, 2 minutes or until a syrup. Add spinach and toss to coat. Season to taste with salt.
6. Serve garnished with toasted pine nuts.

BRUSSELS SPROUTS AND CHICKPEA SALAD

Time: 30 mins | Serves 3
Net carbs: 42g | Fat: 27g
Protein: 19g | Kcal: 455

INGREDIENTS

- 13 g / ½ oz thinly sliced red onion
- 340 g / 12 oz Brussels sprouts, cleaned and halved
- 440 g / 15 ½ oz chickpeas, drained and rinsed
- 3 tbsp virgin olive oil, divided
- 1 lemon
- Freshly ground black pepper
- 55 g / 2 oz sun-dried tomatoes, thinly sliced
- 2 tbsp chopped parsley leaves
- 115 g / 4 oz crumbled feta cheese
- Salt

INSTRUCTIONS

1. Preheat the oven to 205°C / 400°F.
2. In a small bowl of cold water, soak the onion for 10 minutes. Drain and set aside.
3. Grate 2 tsp of the lemon zest and set aside. Squeeze 1-1/2 tbsp juice from the lemon and set aside.
4. In a large bowl, add the Brussels sprouts, chickpeas, oil, lemon zest and ½ tsp pepper, stirring well. On a foil-lined baking sheet, spread the Brussels sprout mixture and roast, tossing once, 15 minutes or until the Brussels sprouts are nicely browned and crisp-tender. Let cool.
5. In a large serving bowl, add the tomatoes, parsley, feta cheese, Brussels sprout and chickpea mixture. Drizzle with the remaining oil and lemon juice, tossing well to coat.
6. Season to taste with salt and pepper. Serve warm.

FATTOUSH

Time: 30 mins | Serves 6-8
Net carbs: 16g | Fat: 7g
Protein: 3g | Kcal: 129

INGREDIENTS

- 2 pitas, split
- 3 tbsp extra-virgin olive oil, divided
- 1 ¼ tsp ground sumac, divided
- 70 ml / 2 ½ oz lemon juice salt
- Freshly ground black pepper
- 1 large head of romaine lettuce, coarsely chopped
- 2 large tomatoes diced
- 1 large cucumber, peeled, seeded and diced
- ½ thinly sliced red onion
- 30 g / 1 oz chopped fresh mint

INSTRUCTIONS

1. Preheat the oven to 175°C / 350°F.
2. Arrange pita halves cut-side up on a baking sheet. Brush with 1 tbsp oil. Sprinkle with 1 tsp sumac. Bake, 15 minutes or until pitas are golden and crisp. Let cool. Break into bite-size pieces.
3. In a large bowl, combine the lettuce, tomatoes, cucumbers, onion, mint, the remaining sumac and the pita pieces.
4. In a small bowl, whisk juice, salt, pepper. Slowly whisk in the remaining oil. Drizzle over lettuce mixture, tossing to coat.
5. Let stand for 15 minutes. Season to taste with salt and pepper. Tossing again before serving.

Sides & Snacks

BRAISED GREEN BEANS WITH MINT AND FETA

Time: 50 mins | Serves 6
Net carbs: 17g | Fat: 10g
Protein: 5g | Kcal: 168

INGREDIENTS

- 3 tbsp virgin olive oil
- 1 onion, finely chopped
- 4 cloves garlic, minced
- 2 tsps dried oregano
- Pinch of red chile flakes
- 455 g / 1 lb green beans, trimmed and cut pieces
- 1/2 tsp baking soda
- 285 ml / 10 oz water
- 410 g / 14 ½ oz diced tomatoes, with juice
- 1 tbsp tomato paste
- 1 tsp salt
- 1/4 tsp freshly ground black pepper
- 2 tbsp chopped fresh mint
- Red wine vinegar
- 55 g / 2 oz crumbled feta cheese

INSTRUCTIONS

1. Preheat the oven to 135°C / 275°F with an oven rack in the lower third.
2. In a Dutch pot over medium heat, add the oil and heat until shimmering. Add onion and cook, stirring often, 3 minutes or until softened. Add garlic, oregano and chili flakes; cook, stirring, 1 minute or until fragrant.
3. Stir in water, baking soda and green beans; cook until simmering. Reduce heat to medium-low and cook, stirring occasionally, for 10 minutes. Stir in tomatoes with juice, tomato paste, salt and pepper.
4. Cover pot and bake, 45 minutes or until beans are tender and sauce is slightly thickened.
5. Add mint and stir in vinegar to taste. Serve sprinkled with feta.

PORCINI MUSHROOM RISOTTO WITH PEAS

Time: 40 mins | Serves 4
Net carbs: 35g | Fat: 5g
Protein: 7g | Kcal: 221

INGREDIENTS

- 570 ml / 20 oz reduced-sodium chicken broth
- 1 tbsp virgin olive oil
- 40 g / 1 ½ oz chopped shallots
- 1 clove garlic, minced
- 50 g / 1 ¾ oz arborio rice
- Salt
- 2 tsp porcini mushroom powder
- 140 ml / 5 oz dry white wine
- 170 g / 6 oz frozen peas, thawed
- 55 g / 2 oz grated low-fat parmesan cheese
- Freshly ground black pepper

INSTRUCTIONS

1. In a medium saucepan over medium heat, add broth and heat until simmering. Reduce heat to low and keep broth steaming but not simmering.
2. In a Dutch pot over medium heat add oil and heat until shimmering. Add the shallots and cook, stirring, 2 minutes or until softened. Add the garlic and cook, stirring, 1 minute or until fragrant.
3. Add rice and 1 tsp salt; cook, stirring, 3 minutes or until rice is coated and turning opaque. Stir in broth and wine; cook, stirring frequently, 25 to 30 minutes or until rice is creamy and al dente and most of the liquid is absorbed. Stir in peas during the last 5 minutes of cooking.
4. Remove from the heat and stir in cheese.
5. Season to taste with salt and pepper. Serve.

SWEET AND SAVORY BASMATI RICE SALAD

Time: 45 mins | Serves 8
Net carbs: 36g | Fat: 12g
Protein: 4g | Kcal: 256

INGREDIENTS

- 200 g / 7 oz basmati rice
- Salt
- 80 g / 3 oz slivered almonds
- 110 g / 4 oz chopped dates
- 4 green onions, thinly sliced
- 33 g / 1 oz chopped fresh parsley leaves
- 2-1/2 tbsp lemon juice
- 1 tsp grated orange zest plus 2 tbsp juice from
- 1 orange
- 1/2 tsp ground cinnamon
- Freshly ground black pepper
- 70 ml / 2 ½ oz extra virgin olive oil

INSTRUCTIONS

1. In a medium skillet over medium heat, add rice and cook, stirring often, 7 minutes or until fragrant and grains are just turning opaque.
2. Bring a large pot of water to a boil. Stir in 2 tsp salt and the rice; cook, uncovered, 9 to 11 minutes or until rice is tender. Drain rice, transfer the rice to a baking sheet and spread out
3. The rice. Let stand, 20 minutes or until cooled completely.
4. Meanwhile, in the medium skillet over medium heat, add the almonds and cook, shaking, 3 minutes or until fragrant and lightly toasted. Set aside to cool.
5. Transfer rice to a large serving bowl. Stir in dates, onions and parsley.
6. In a medium bowl, whisk together lemon juice, 2 tbsp orange juice, 1 tsp orange zest, cinnamon and 1/4 tsp pepper. Slowly whisk in oil. Season with salt and pepper to taste.
7. Drizzle over the rice mixture and toss to combine. Let stand for 20 minutes. Serve.

SIMPLE LEBANESE RICE

Time: 35 mins | Serves 6
Net carbs: 77g | Fat: 7g
Protein: 49g | Kcal: 415

INGREDIENTS

- 400 g / 14 oz long-grain rice, rinsed and drained
- 140 g / 5 oz broken vermicelli pasta
- 2 tbsp virgin olive oil
- Salt
- 70 g / 2 ½ oz toasted pine nuts (optional)

INSTRUCTIONS

1. In a medium bowl, add the rice and cover it with water. Let stand for 15 minutes; drain.
2. In a medium, heavy-bottom saucepan over medium-high heat, add the oil and heat until shimmering. Add the vermicelli and cook, stirring, 2 minutes or until golden brown. Add the rice, stirring, 2 minutes or until rice is coated in oil. Season with salt. Stir in 850 ml of water. Bring to a boil.
3. Reduce heat to low, cover and cook, 15 minutes or until rice is al dente and water is absorbed. Remove from heat, cover and let stand for 5 minutes.
4. Remove cover and fluff rice with a fork. Spoon rice into a serving bowl. Serve garnished with toasted pine nuts, if using.

TABBOULEH

Time: 3 hrs 35 mins | Serves 4
Net carbs: 18g | Fat: 15g
Protein: 5g | Kcal: 202

INGREDIENTS

- 35 g / 1 ¼ oz fine bulgur wheat
- 225 g / ½ lb tomatoes, finely chopped
- 1 bunch green onions, thinly sliced
- 180 g / 6 ⅓ oz chopped fresh flat-leaf parsley
- 10 g / ⅓ oz chopped fresh mint
- 1 clove garlic, minced
- 2 lemons, juice of
- Salt
- 3 tbsp extra virgin olive oil
- 1 large head of romaine lettuce, coarsely chopped

INSTRUCTIONS

1. In a medium bowl, add the bulgur and cover it with water. Let stand for 20 minutes or until slightly softened. Using a fine-mesh strainer lined with cheesecloth, drain bulgur, pressing down to squeeze out water.
2. Transfer bulgur to a large bowl. Add the tomatoes, onions, parsley, mint, garlic and juice tossing to combine. Season to taste with salt. Cover and refrigerate for 2 to 3 hours or until the bulgur absorbs more liquids and swells.
3. Drizzle in the olive oil, tossing well. Season to taste with salt. Add the lettuce, tossing to coat. Let stand for 15 minutes. Serve.

CAULIFLOWER COUSCOUS

Time: 10 mins | Serves 4
Net carbs: 66g | Fat: 11g
Protein: 11g | Kcal: 202

INGREDIENTS

- 170 g / 6 oz couscous
- 3 tbsp virgin olive oil
- 70 g / 2 ½ oz cauliflower florets
- 1 shallot, sliced
- Salt
- Freshly ground black pepper
- 40 g / 1 ½ oz chopped dates
- Pinch cinnamon
- 30 g / 1 oz firmly packed chopped parsley
- 1 tbsp red wine vinegar

INSTRUCTIONS

1. Cook couscous according to the package directions. Drain and rinse with cold water. Transfer to a large bowl and toss with 1 tbsp olive oil.
2. In a large skillet, add remaining oil and heat until shimmering. Add cauliflower and shallots; cook, stirring often, 6 minutes. Season with salt and pepper. Stir in dates and cinnamon and cook, stirring often, 2 minutes or until cauliflower is crisp-tender and flavors are melded.
3. Stir cauliflower mixture, parsley and vinegar into couscous.
4. Season to taste with salt and pepper. Serve.

LEBANESE POTATOES

Time: 20 mins | Serves 4
Net carbs: 33g | Fat: 11g
Protein: 4g | Kcal: 237

INGREDIENTS

- 680 g / 1 ½ lbs red potatoes, scrubbed and cut into chunks
- 3 tbsp olive oil
- 2 tbsp minced garlic
- 8 ½ g / ⅓ oz minced cilantro
- 1 ¾ tbsp paprika
- 1 tsp cayenne
- Salt
- 2 tbsp minced parsley
- 2 tbsp fresh lemon juice

INSTRUCTIONS

1. Rinse potatoes in cold water until water runs clear. Bring a pot of salted water to a boil. Add potatoes and boil for 5 minutes or until they begin to soften and become slightly translucent. Drain and let completely air dry completely on paper towels.
2. In a saucepan, add 2 tbsp oil and garlic; cook over medium-low heat, covered, 3 minutes or until softened and pale gold. Add the cilantro and cook, stirring, 1 to 2 minutes or until wilted. Transfer sauce to a large bowl and set aside.
3. In a large skillet over medium heat, add remaining oil and heat until shimmering. Add the potatoes and cook, flipping occasionally (do not stir), 5 to 7 minutes or until browned and crispy on all sides.
4. Transfer potatoes to the bowl of sauce. Sprinkle it with paprika and cayenne. Season with salt and toss gently. Transfer mixture to a serving bowl. Garnish with parsley. Serve drizzled with lemon juice. Serve warm.

ROASTED VEGETABLES WITH GARLIC AND THYME

Time: 1 hr 30 mins | Serves 8
Net carbs: 22g | Fat: 6g
Protein: 5g | Kcal: 146

INGREDIENTS

- 3 tbsp olive oil
- 4 medium red beets
- 680 g / 1 1/2 lbs carrots, peeled and cut into thick rounds
- 680 g / 1 1/2 lbs Brussels sprouts, trimmed and halved lengthwise
- 8 large cloves garlic, unpeeled
- 1 tbsp chopped fresh thyme
- Salt
- Freshly ground black pepper

INSTRUCTIONS

1. Preheat the oven to 190°C / 375°F.
2. Cut greens from beets. Do not cut the root end. Scrub beets well.
3. Brush beets all over with 1 tbsp oil. Arrange the beets in a square glass baking dish and cover them with foil. Roast 30 minutes.
4. Meanwhile, arrange the carrots, Brussels sprouts and garlic in a large glass baking dish. Toss with the remaining oil, 3/4 tsp salt and 1/4 tsp pepper.
5. Keep the beets in the oven. Add the carrot mixture to the oven and roast, stirring occasionally, 60 minutes or until vegetables are fork-tender.
6. Transfer the beets to a cutting board. Let cool.
7. Stir the thyme into the carrot mixture and continue roasting for another 10 minutes.
8. When the beets are cool enough to handle, peel and cut them into chunks. Transfer beets to a serving bowl.
9. Add the carrot mixture to the beets, tossing well. Season to taste with salt and pepper. Serve.

FETA DILL DIP

Time: 30 mins | Serves 2
Net carbs: 3g | Fat: 2g
Protein: 1g | Kcal: 28

INGREDIENTS

- 245 g / 8 ½ oz plain full-fat Greek yogurt
- 85 g / 3 oz feta cheese
- 1 medium clove garlic, halved
- 1 tbsp fresh lemon juice
- 2 tbsp chopped dill
- 1 ½ tsp grated lemon zest
- Salt
- Freshly ground black pepper

INSTRUCTIONS

In a food processor, add the yogurt, cheese, garlic, lemon juice, lemon zest and dill. Process until almost smooth. Season to taste with salt and pepper. Let stand for 30 minutes. Serve.

FRUIT, NUT AND SEED BARS

Time: 30 mins | Serves 18
Net carbs: 31g | Fat: 10g
Protein: 4g | Kcal: 217

INGREDIENTS

- 180 g / 6 ⅓ oz old-fashioned rolled oats
- 150 g / 5 ⅓ oz nuts (for example almonds, pecans, walnuts or pistachios)
- 200 g / 7 oz dried fruits, (for example cranberries, cherries, raisins or dates)
- 170 g / 6 oz honey
- 1/4 tsp salt
- 70 g / 2.5 oz unsweetened shredded coconut
- 65 g / 2 ⅓ oz seeds (for example pumpkin, sunflower, sesame or flax)
- 1 tbsp butter

INSTRUCTIONS

1. Preheat the oven to 220°C / 425°F.
2. Arrange oats and nuts on a rimmed baking sheet. Bake for 7 minutes or until nicely toasted. Let cool slightly.
3. Transfer mixture to a food processor. Add dried fruits, honey and salt; pulse to combine, leaving some pieces coarsely chopped. Add coconut and seed; pulsing to combine.
4. Spray a baking pan with nonstick cooking spray. Line the pan with foil and coat with butter. Press mixture firmly into the pan.
5. Bake for 20 minutes or until browned and firm. Cool completely.
6. Using the edges of the foil, remove bars from the pan. Using a serrated knife, cut into bars.
7. Bars can be stored in an airtight container, separated by parchment paper, for up to 2 weeks

EASY CREAMY HUMMUS

Time: 35 mins | Serves 8
Net carbs: 32g | Fat: 13g
Protein: 11g | Kcal: 266

INGREDIENTS

- 255 g / 9 oz dried chickpeas, rinsed and drained
- 1 tsp baking soda
- 2 L water
- 70 ml fresh lemon juice
- 60 g / 2 oz tahini
- 3 tbsp extra virgin olive oil
- 1 clove garlic, minced
- 1/2 tsp ground cumin
- 3 tbsp water
- Salt
- Ground paprika

INSTRUCTIONS

1. In a large bowl, combine chickpeas and water. Let stand at room temperature for 8 hours or overnight. Drain and rinse.
2. In a large stockpot over high heat, add the chickpeas and baking soda; cook, stirring, 3 minutes. Add the water and heat until boiling. Reduce heat to simmer and cook, skimming off any foam or skins, 10 to 40 minutes or until tender, checking doneness every 5 minutes after the first 10 minutes. Drain and rinse.
3. In a food processor, add the tahini and lemon juice; process, scraping down the sides, for 90 seconds or until creamy. Add 2 tbsp oil, garlic, cumin and 1/2 tsp salt; process, scraping the sides, 1 minute or until blended.
4. Add half of the chickpeas and process, scraping the sides, for 1 minute. Add the remaining chickpeas and process, scraping the sides, 2 minutes or until smooth. Add water, 1 tbsp at a time, and process until desired consistency.
5. Transfer to a serving bowl. Season to taste with salt. Using the back of a spoon, make a swirled indentation on top of the hummus and drizzle with oil. Serve garnished with paprika.

Meat

MEDITERRANEAN STUFFED CHICKEN

Time: 35 mins | Serves 3
Net carbs: 14g | Fat: 25g
Protein: 28g | Kcal: 393

INGREDIENTS

- 50 g / 1 ¾ oz crumbled feta cheese
- 3 sun-dried tomatoes (in oil), drained and diced
- 3 tbsp finely chopped walnuts
- 4 black olives, chopped
- 1 lemon, zest and juice
- 2 tsp ground oregano
- 2 boneless skinless chicken breasts
- 8 fresh basil leaves
- 1 tsp extra-virgin olive oil
- Salt
- Freshly ground black pepper

INSTRUCTIONS

1. Preheat the oven to 205°C / 400°F.
2. In a small bowl, combine the feta cheese, tomatoes, walnuts, olives, 2 tsp lemon zest, 2 tsp lemon juice and oregano. Set aside.
3. Place 3 to 4 basil leaves on each breast, leaving space from the edges.
4. Spoon half of the cheese mixture in the center of each breast.
5. Starting with the narrower end, roll the breast up tightly. Use 2 to 3 toothpicks to
6. secure rolls. Brush roll-ups with oil. Season with salt and pepper
7. Bake for 25 minutes or until an instant-read thermometer inserted into the thickest part registers 75°C / 165°F and the chicken is no longer pink inside.

CHICKEN, PEPPERS AND RED ONION KEBABS

Time: 45 mins | Serves 6
Net carbs: 6g | Fat: 25g
Protein: 39g | Kcal: 410

INGREDIENTS

- 3 large cloves garlic, crushed
- 3 tbsp finely chopped fresh rosemary leaves
- 1 ½ tbsp finely chopped fresh oregano
- 2 tsp salt
- ½ tsp freshly ground black pepper
- 6 tbsp olive oil
- 70 ml / 2 ½ oz fresh lemon juice
- 680 g / 1 ½ lb boneless skinless chicken breasts, cut into pieces
- 1 red bell pepper, cut into pieces
- 1 red onion, cut into wedges

INSTRUCTIONS

1. In a large bowl, combine garlic, rosemary, oregano, 1 tsp salt, pepper, 5 tbsp oil and 3 tbsp juice. Add chicken, tossing to coat in the marinade. Cover and refrigerate for 30 minutes or up to an hour.
2. Meanwhile, soak a wooden skewer in water for about 30 minutes.
3. Preheat the oven to 220°C / 425°F.
4. In a small bowl, combine the remaining lemon juice, oil and salt. Thread chicken, peppers and onions onto skewers, alternating as desired. Discard marinade.
5. Arrange skewers on a foil-lined baking sheet with a rack. Baste skewer with lemon mixture. Bake, turning occasionally and basting with lemon mixture, 12 minutes or until chicken is no longer pink in the middle and vegetables are tender. Discard the remaining lemon mixture.

BRAISED CHICKEN BREASTS WITH BULGUR PILAF

Time: 20 mins | Serves 4
Net carbs: 13g | Fat: 26g
Protein: 32g | Kcal: 403

INGREDIENTS

- 4 boneless, skinless chicken breasts
- Salt
- Freshly ground black pepper
- 100 ml / 3 ½ oz virgin olive oil
- 140 g / 5 oz fine-grind bulgur
- 180g / 10 oz cherry tomatoes, halved
- 90 g / 3 ¼ oz pitted black olives, halved
- 115 g / 4 oz feta cheese, crumbled
- 45 g / 1 ½ oz minced fresh parsley
- 1 tbsp fresh lemon juice

INSTRUCTIONS

1. Season chicken with salt and pepper. In a large skillet over medium-high heat, add 1 tbsp oil and heat until shimmering. Cook breasts, turning once, 8 minutes or until browned and no longer pink in the middle. Transfer chicken to a cutting board and tent with foil.
2. Add 425 ml / 15 oz water to the skillet and cook, scraping up any browned bits from the bottom of the pan, until the mixture begins to boil. Stir in 2 tsp salt and bulgur. Remove from the heat. Cover and let it stand for 5 minutes, or until bulgur is al dente.
3. Fluff bulgur with a fork. Stir in tomatoes, olives, feta, parsley, lemon juice and 2 tbsp oil. Season to taste with salt and pepper.
4. Slice chicken across the grain. Spoon bulgur onto serving plates. Arrange chicken on and around bulgur. Serve drizzled with remaining oil.

HERB ROASTED LAMB CHOPS

Time: 25 mins | Serves 4
Net carbs: 1g | Fat: 39g
Protein: 36g | Kcal: 498

INGREDIENTS

- 3 tbsp extra-virgin olive oil
- 8 lamb chops
- 2 cloves garlic, cut into small slices
- Salt
- 2 tbsp fresh rosemary leaves

INSTRUCTIONS

1. Preheat the oven to 190°C / 375°F.
2. Place chops on a rack on a baking sheet. Brush chops with olive oil. Cut 1 small, shallow slit in the top of each lamb chop. Place a sliver of garlic in each cut. Season lamb with salt and sprinkle with rosemary.
3. Roast chops for 20 minutes or until an instant-read thermometer inserted in the thickest part of the chop registers 75°C / 165°F for medium. Serve warm.

BRAISED LAMB SHANKS

Time: 1 hr 40 mins | Serves 8
Net carbs: 7g | Fat: 35g
Protein: 44g | Kcal: 522

INGREDIENTS

- 4 meaty lamb shanks, trimmed
- Salt
- 2 tsp ground cinnamon
- 1 tsp grated nutmeg
- 1 tsp ground cardamom
- 1 tsp freshly ground black pepper
- 1 tsp turmeric
- Vegetable oil
- 4 tsp crumbled saffron
- 2 limes, zest and juice
- 1 large onion roughly chopped
- 1 orange, zest of
- 3 fresh thyme sprigs
- 2 bay leaves
- 1.7 L / 60 oz hot chicken broth or water
- 2 tbsp coarsely chopped parsley
- 2 tbsp coarsely chopped dill

INSTRUCTIONS

1. Season shanks with salt. In a small bowl, combine cinnamon, nutmeg, cardamom, black pepper and turmeric. Sprinkle mixture over shanks and rub in. Wrap shanks in plastic wrap and refrigerate for 8 hours or overnight.
2. In a large Dutch pot over medium-high heat, add 2.5 cm / ½ inch of oil and heat until shimmering.
3. Working in batches, add lamb shanks and cook, turning frequently, 5 minutes or until browned all over. Transfer to a plate and repeat with remaining shanks.
4. Meanwhile, in a small bowl combine saffron, lime juice and 140 ml / 5 oz warm water. Set aside.
5. Preheat the oven to 175°C / 350°F.
6. Discard all but 2 tbsp oil from the Dutch pot. Over medium heat add onion and cook,
7. stirring often, 7 to 9 minutes or until softened and lightly browned. Season onion with salt. Stir in the zest of 1 lime, orange zest, thyme. Bay leaves and saffron mixture. Arrange shanks in the Dutch pot and pour in broth. Heating until boiling. Cover pot and bake for about 1 1/2 hours or until an instant-read thermometer registers 75°C / 165°F when inserted into the thickest part of the shank for medium and meat is beginning to fall off the bone.
8. Transfer shanks to a large shallow dish and cover with foil. Strain liquid through a fine-mesh sieve into a small saucepan. Discard onions, thyme and bay leaves. Skim fat from liquids. Season to taste with salt. Cook juices over medium heat until warmed through. Meanwhile, remove the lamb from the bones and break it into large chunks. Discard bones. Transfer lamb to individual wide serving bowls. Ladle juices into bowls. Serve garnished with parsley and dill.

SIRLOIN RIBBONS

Time: 2 hrs 35 mins | Serves 4
Net carbs: 2g | Fat: 17g
Protein: 47g | Kcal: 342

INGREDIENTS

- 450 g / 1 ¼ lb sirloin steak, cut into strips
- 3 cloves garlic, mashed
- 2 tsp dried oregano
- 2 tsp salt
- ½ tsp freshly ground black pepper
- 1 tbsp virgin olive oil
- 1 tbsp red wine vinegar

INSTRUCTIONS

1. In a glass baking dish, add the garlic, oregano, salt, pepper, oil and vinegar, mixing well.
2. Add the steak strips, tossing to coat in the marinade. Cover and refrigerate for about 2 hours.
3. Meanwhile, soak wooden skewers in water for about 30 minutes.
4. Preheat broiler with oven rack 13 cm / 5 inches from the top.
5. Weave steak onto skewers. Arrange skewers on a foil-lined baking sheet with a rack.
6. Broil, turning once, about 3 minutes or until nicely browned.
7. Transfer skewer to plates and serve immediately.

ROASTED GARLIC DIJON PORK LOIN

Time: 1 hr 10 mins | Serves 6-8
Net carbs: 1g | Fat: 9g
Protein: 99g | Kcal: 284

INGREDIENTS

- 2 ½ tbsp virgin olive oil, divided
- 1 pork loin roast
- Salt
- Freshly ground black pepper
- 2 tbsp minced garlic
- 1 tbsp crushed oregano leaves
- 1 tbsp Dijon mustard

INSTRUCTIONS

1. Preheat the oven to 175°C / 350°F.
2. In a large skillet over medium-high heat, add 1 tbsp oil and heat until shimmering. Season pork with salt and pepper. Add pork to the skillet and cook, turning occasionally, 8 to 10 minutes or until browned on all sides.
3. Meanwhile, in a small bowl, add 2 tsp oil, garlic, oregano, mustard, ½ tsp salt and ½ tsp pepper, blending well into a paste.
4. Brush paste all over pork. Transfer pork to a foil-line baking sheet.
5. Roast pork for 45 minutes or until a thermometer inserted horizontally into the roast registers 65°C / 145°F for medium-rare to medium. Transfer pork to a cutting board, cover with foil and let stand for 10 minutes.
6. Slice pork across the grain. Transfer to a serving platter and serve immediately.

PORK CHOPS WITH VEGETABLE MEDLEY

Time: 20 mins | Serves 4
Net carbs: 102g | Fat: 16g
Protein: 19g | Kcal: 258

INGREDIENTS

- 4 boneless rib pork chops
- Salt
- Freshly ground black pepper
- 2 tbsp olive oil
- 2 medium zucchini, cut into pieces
- 3 cloves garlic, minced
- 215 ml / 7 ½ oz low-sodium chicken broth
- 1 tbsp chopped fresh oregano
- 300 g / 10 ½ oz cherry tomatoes, halved
- 60 g / 2 oz pitted black olives, halved

INSTRUCTIONS

1. Season pork chops with salt and pepper. In a large skillet, add 1 tbsp oil and cook over medium-high heat until shimmering. Add pork chops and cook, turning once, 7 minutes until browned and pink in the center. Transfer chops to a plate and cover with foil.
2. Add remaining oil to the skillet and heat until shimmering. Add zucchini and season with salt; cook, stirring often, about 4 minutes until browned. Add garlic and cook, stirring, 1 minute. Add broth and oregano; cook, scraping up any browned bits from the bottom of the pan, 1 minute. Move zucchini to the edges of the pan. Return chops and any accumulated juices to pan; cook, turning chops occasionally, 7 minutes or until pork is no longer pink in the middle and sauce is slightly thickened. Transfer chops to a serving platter.
3. Add tomatoes and olives to the skillet and cook, tossing gently, 1 minute or until warmed through. Season to taste with salt and pepper. Spoon vegetable mixture over the chops. Serve warm.

PAELLA VALENCIANA

Time: 40 mins | Serves 8
Net carbs: 38g | Fat: 15g
Protein: 59g | Kcal: 517

INGREDIENTS

- 3 tbsp virgin olive oil
- 1 whole chicken, cut into 8 pieces
- 1 small onion cut into slices
- 4 medium tomatoes, each cut into 6 wedges
- 1 tbsp paprika
- 1 tbsp salt
- ½ tsp freshly ground black pepper
- ¼ tsp cayenne pepper
- 3 saffron threads
- 300 g / 10 ½ oz arborio rice
- 850 ml / 30 oz chicken broth
- 450 g / 1 lb large shrimp, peeled and deveined
- 240 g / 8 ½ oz frozen peas
- 115 g / 4 oz sliced pimiento, drained

INSTRUCTIONS

1. In a large Dutch pot or Paella pan over medium heat, add 2 tbsp oil and heat until shimmering. Working in batches, add chicken and cook, turning, 6 to 8 minutes or until browned all over. Transfer chicken to a plate, adding oil as necessary between batches.
2. Add onions and tomatoes to the Dutch pot; cook, stirring often, 5 minutes or until onion is softened.
3. Stir in paprika, salt, black pepper, cayenne pepper, saffron, rice and broth. Add chicken, cover and simmer for 20 minutes.
4. Gently stir in shrimp and peas. Cook, stirring often, 10 minutes or until shrimp are pink, firm and opaque and peas are tender. Gently stir in pimiento and cook until heated through. Serve immediately.

Fish & Seafood

LEMON GARLIC BAKED COD

Time: 30 mins | Serves 4
Net carbs: 5g | Fat: 15g
Protein: 31g | Kcal: 280

INGREDIENTS

- 4 115 g / 6 oz pieces cod fillets
- Kosher salt
- Freshly ground black
- pepper
- 2 lemons
- 3 tbsp virgin olive oil
- 3 cloves garlic, minced
- 1 tsp paprika
- 1 tsp ground coriander
- 3/4 tsp ground cumin
- 1/8 tsp cayenne pepper
- 15 g / 1/2 oz chopped fresh parsley leaves

INSTRUCTIONS

1. Preheat the oven to 205°C / 400°F with a rack in the middle of the oven.
2. Brush cod fillet with olive oil and arrange in a glass baking dish with space in-between. Season with salt and pepper.
3. Squeeze 4 tbsp lemon juice and grate 1/2 tsp zest from lemons. Cut the remaining lemon into wedges. Set aside.
4. In a small saucepan over medium heat, add the remaining oil and heat until shimmering. Add the garlic and cook, stirring, 30 seconds or until fragrant. Remove from the heat and stir in the lemon juice, paprika, coriander, cumin and cayenne. Pour mixture over fillets.
5. Bake, basting occasionally, 10 to 15 minutes or until the fish is opaque and flakes easily when tested with a fork.
6. Transfer fillets to serving plates and spoon liquids from the baking dish over the top. Sprinkle with parsley. Serve garnished with lemon wedges.

HERB ROASTED SEA BASS

Time: 20 mins | Serves 2
Net carbs: 7g | Fat: 14g
Protein: 27g | Kcal: 255

INGREDIENTS

- 1 lemon, halved
- 5 tsp extra virgin olive oil
- 2 tsp lemon juice
- ½ tsp dried oregano
- 2 cloves garlic
- Kosher salt
- Freshly ground black pepper
- 2 140 g / 5 oz skinless sea bass fillets

INSTRUCTIONS

1. Preheat the oven to 245°C / 475°F.
2. In a small bowl, squeeze 2 tsp lemon juice from one half. Set aside the remaining half. Whisk in 3 tsp oil and oregano. Season with salt and pepper. Set aside.
3. Brush a glass baking dish with the remaining oil.
4. Arrange fish in a prepared dish, turning to coat in oil. Season fish with salt and pepper. Place garlic around the fish. Spoon ½ tbsp lemon mixture over fish.
5. Bake fish, 12 minutes or until fish is opaque and flakes easily when tested with a fork. Let the fish stand for 5 minutes.
6. Meanwhile, cut the remaining lemon half into wedges. Transfer fish to serving plates and top
7. with remaining sauce. Arrange lemon wedges around fish. Serve immediately.

BAKED SNAPPER WITH TOMATOES AND OLIVES

Time: 15 mins | Serves 4
Net carbs: 6g | Fat: 14g
Protein: 30g | Kcal: 280

INGREDIENTS

- 3 tbsp virgin olive oil
- 4 140 g / 5 oz pieces snapper fillet
- Fine sea salt
- Freshly ground black pepper
- ½ tsp ground fennel
- 90 g / 3 ¼ oz pitted black olives
- 2 tbsp dry white wine
- 450 g / 1 lb tomatoes, seeded and cut into pieces
- 5 g / ¼ oz lightly packed torn fresh basil leaves

INSTRUCTIONS

1. Preheat the oven to 205°C / 400°F.
2. In a glass baking dish add the oil. Heat oil in the oven until it shimmers.
3. Cut a few shallow slits into the skin of each fillet.
4. Season fillets with salt, pepper and fennel.
5. Place the fish in the baking dish skin-side down to coat in the oil and immediately flip over to skin-side up. Scatter olives around the fish. Drizzle with wine.
6. Bake for 6 to 8 minutes or until the fish is opaque and flakes easily when tested with a fork.
7. Season tomatoes with salt and pepper. Scatter tomatoes around fish, about 2 minutes before the end of the roasting time.
8. Serve fish immediately with olives and tomatoes scattered around the fish.

LEMON-HERB SALMON WITH SICILIAN CAPONATA

Time: 40 mins | Serves 4
Net carbs: 20g | Fat: 20g
Protein: 31g | Kcal: 373

INGREDIENTS

- 1 medium eggplant, cut into pieces
- 1 red bell pepper, cut into pieces
- 1 summer squash, cut into pieces
- 1 small onion, cut into pieces
- 225 g / 8 oz cherry tomatoes
- 3 tbsp virgin olive oil
- 1 tsp salt, divided
- ½ tsp ground black pepper, divided
- 2 tbsp capers, rinsed and chopped
- 1 tbsp red wine vinegar
- 2 tsp honey
- 4 140 g / 5 oz salmon fillets
- 1 lemon
- ½ tsp Italian seasoning

INSTRUCTIONS

1. Preheat the oven to 230°C / 450°F with racks in the upper and lower thirds of the oven. Line 2 rimmed baking sheets with foil and spray with nonstick cooking spray.
2. Meanwhile, in a large bowl, add eggplant, bell pepper, squash, onion, tomatoes, oil, ¾ tsp salt and ¼ tsp pepper; toss well. Divide the mixture between the prepared baking sheets and roast on the upper and lower racks, stirring once halfway through cooking, 25 minutes or until the vegetables are tender and lightly browned.
3. Return vegetables to the large bowl and stir in capers, vinegar and honey. Set aside.
4. Grate lemon zest and measure 1 tsp. Cut the remaining lemon into wedges and set aside.
5. Place salmon on one of the baking sheets. Sprinkle salmon with zest, Italian seasoning and the remaining salt and pepper.
6. Place pan on the lower rack and roast for 9 minutes or until the salmon is opaque and flakes easily when tested with a fork.
7. Transfer salmon to serving plates and spoon the caponata alongside. Serve with lemon wedges.

BAKED LUMP CRAB CAKES

Time: 45 mins | Serves 6
Net carbs: 5g | Fat: 15g
Protein: 19g | Kcal: 234

INGREDIENTS

- 1 lemon, cut into 8 wedges
- 1 egg
- 115 g / 4 oz real mayonnaise
- 1 tsp Worcestershire sauce
- 1 tsp Dijon mustard
- 1 tsp seafood seasoning, preferably Old Bay
- ¼ tsp cayenne pepper
- Pinch salt
- 450 g / 1 ½ lb lump crab meat
- 15 g / ½ oz chopped fresh parsley
- 2 green onions, thinly sliced
- 55 g / 2 oz bread crumbs
- Pickled red onions
- Watercress
- Mandarin orange slices

INSTRUCTIONS

1. Line a baking sheet with parchment paper. Set aside.
2. In a large bowl, squeeze 1 tsp lemon juice (about 2 lemon wedges). Set aside the remaining lemon wedges.
3. In the same bowl, whisk in the egg, mayonnaise, Worcestershire sauce, mustard, seafood seasoning, cayenne and salt. Gently stir in crab, parsley and onions. Fold in bread crumbs until just combined.
4. Gently form crab mixture into 12 balls, without squeezing, and arrange on a pre-prepared baking sheet. Gently press balls into thick patties. Refrigerate for 30 minutes.
5. Preheat the oven to 205°C / 400°F.
6. Bake crab cakes for 12 to 15 minutes or until the tops are light golden brown and an instant-read thermometer registers 75°C / 165° F.
7. Transfer to serving plates. Serve garnished with lemon wedges, pickled onions, watercress, and orange slices.

BAKED TUNA STEAKS WITH GARLIC AIOLI

Time: 20 mins | Serves 4
Net carbs: 2g | Fat: 25g
Protein: 34g | Kcal: 371

INGREDIENTS

Aioli
- 2 cloves garlic, smashed
- 125 g / 4 ½ oz Greek yogurt
- 2 tbsp extra virgin olive oil
- 1 tbsp fresh lemon juice
- Salt
- Freshly ground black pepper

Tuna
- 2 tbsp chopped fresh basil
- 70 ml / 2 ½ oz virgin olive oil
- ¼ tsp garlic powder
- 4 tuna steaks

INSTRUCTIONS

1. Preheat the oven to 230°C / 450°F.
2. Aioli: Using a mortar and pestle, mash garlic and ¼ tsp salt until a paste. In a small bowl, add yogurt, oil, juice and garlic paste, whisking until blended. Season to taste with salt and pepper. Cover and refrigerate.
3. Tuna: In another small bowl, add basil, oil and garlic powder. Season with salt and pepper.
4. Line a rimmed baking sheet with foil. Brush tuna with basil oil mixture. Bake the tuna 8 to 12 minutes or until tuna flakes easily when tested with a fork but is slightly pink in the middle.
5. Transfer tuna to serving plates. Serve with a large dollop of aioli.

Pasta

HEARTY LASAGNA WITH LENTILS AND ZUCCHINI

Time: 1 hr 10 mins | Serves 8
Net carbs: 48g | Fat: 8g
Protein: 19g | Kcal: 331

INGREDIENTS

- 200 g / 7 oz dry whole lentils, rinsed
- 850 ml / 30 oz water
- 1 ¼ tsp fennel seeds
- 440 g / 15 ½ oz low-sodium tomato sauce
- ⅛ tsp granulated sugar
- 1 tsp dried basil leaves, crushed
- 1 tsp salt
- 225 g / 8 oz whole-grain lasagna noodles
- 2 tbsp virgin olive oil
- 50 g / 1 ¾ oz chopped onion
- 3 large cloves garlic, minced
- 2 zucchini, sliced
- 225 g / 8 oz low-fat shredded mozzarella cheese

INSTRUCTIONS

1. In a large pot, combine the lentils, water and fennel seeds. Bring to a boil, reduce the heat, cover, and simmer for 15 to 20 minutes, or until the lentils are tender. Drain. Stir in the tomato sauce, sugar, basil and salt. Set aside.
2. Cook noodles according to the package directions.
3. Preheat the oven to 175°C / 350°F.
4. In a large skillet over medium heat and 1½ tbsp of oil and heat until shimmering. Add the onions and cook, stirring often, 5 to 7 minutes or until softened. Add the garlic and cook, stirring, 1 minute or until the garlic is fragrant. Transfer mixture to a bowl and set aside.
5. Add the remaining oil to the skillet and heat over medium heat until shimmering. Add the zucchini and cook, turning, 8 minutes or until the zucchini are just tender.
6. Lightly oil a glass baking dish. Arrange half of the lasagna noodles on the bottom of the dish. Layer the zucchini, half of the lentils and cheese. Layer the remaining noodles, the onion mixture and the remaining lentils.
7. Cover with foil and bake for 30 minutes or until heated through. Uncover and sprinkle with the remaining cheese. Bake, uncovered, 5 minutes or until the cheese is melted and golden brown.

WHOLE GRAIN LASAGNA WITH EGGPLANT AND OLIVES

Time: 30 mins | Serves 6
Net carbs: 40g | Fat: 14g
Protein: 12g | Kcal: 324

INGREDIENTS

- 6 whole-grain lasagna sheets
- 70 g / 2 ½ oz olive oil
- 2 small eggplant, peeled and diced
- 1 onion, diced
- 2 small carrots, diced
- 1 red bell pepper, seeded and diced
- 18 black olives, pitted and finely chopped
- 2 cloves garlic, minced
- 1 tbsp finely chopped fresh cilantro leaves
- ¼ tsp salt
- 70 ml / 2 ½ oz water
- 225 g / 8 oz shredded low-fat mozzarella cheese
- 170 g / 6 oz tomato sauce

INSTRUCTIONS

1. Preheat the oven to 175°C / 350°F.
2. Cook the lasagna al dente according to package directions. Drain and rinse with cool water. Let cool.
3. In a large sauté pan over medium heat, add the oil and heat until shimmering. Add the eggplant, onion, carrot, bell pepper, olives, garlic, cilantro, salt and water; cook, stirring occasionally, 8 minutes or until the vegetables are tender.
4. Spoon about 2 tbsp of the eggplant mixture and 4 tsp of the mozzarella down the middle of each noodle. Starting with the end closest to you, roll each noodle up and then secure it with a toothpick.
5. In a greased glass baking dish, arrange the rollups. Spoon the tomato sauce over the top. Sprinkle it with the remaining cheese.
6. Bake for 15 to 20 minutes or until the cheese is golden brown.

PASTA PRIMAVERA

Time: 20 mins | Serves 8
Net carbs: 54g | Fat: 10g
Protein: 14g | Kcal: 373

INGREDIENTS

- 450 g / 1 lb whole grain fettuccine
- 3 tbsp virgin olive oil
- 689 g / 1 ½ lb asparagus, trimmed and cut into pieces
- 2 carrots, thinly sliced
- 70 g / 2 ½ oz small broccoli florets
- 340 g / 12 oz frozen peas
- 3 onions, chopped
- 30 g / 1 oz lightly packed baby spinach leaves

Sauce:
- 425 ml / 15 oz vegetable broth
- 70 ml / 2 ½ oz dry white wine
- 120 g / 4 ¼ oz crème fraîche
- 50 g / 1 ¾ oz grated Parmigiano-Reggiano
- 1/2 lemon, juice
- Salt
- Freshly ground black pepper
- Fresh parsley leaves

INSTRUCTIONS

1. Cook fettuccine according to the package directions. Drain pasta. Transfer to a large bowl and toss with 2 tbsp oil. Set aside.
2. In a large skillet over medium heat, add the remaining oil and heat until shimmering. Add the asparagus, carrots and broccoli; cook, stirring often, 5 minutes or until the vegetables begin to soften. Stir in the peas, onions and spinach; cook, stirring often, 3 minutes. Transfer the vegetables to a large bowl.
3. In the same skillet over medium heat, add the broth and wine; cook for 3 to 4 minutes until the liquid has reduced by half. Stir in the crème fraîche, Parmigiano-Reggiano and lemon juice. Season to taste with salt and pepper. Add the vegetable mixture to the sauce and simmer, stirring often, 3 minutes or until flavors are melded. Pour mixture over the fettuccine, tossing to coat.
4. Serve garnished with parsley.

TUSCAN BAKED ZITI

Time: 30 mins | Serves 6
Net carbs: 76g | Fat: 10g
Protein: 21g | Kcal: 489

INGREDIENTS

- 300 g / 10 ½ oz whole-grain ziti pasta
- 225 g / 8 oz shredded Italian cheese blend, divided
- 2 red bell peppers, cored, seeded and cut into strips
- 2 zucchini, halved lengthwise and sliced crosswise
- 225 g / 8 oz sliced fresh button mushrooms
- 680 g / 24 oz pasta sauce
- 1 tbsp chopped fresh oregano leaves

INSTRUCTIONS

1. Preheat the oven to 190°C / 375°F.
2. Cook pasta according to package directions. Drain and transfer to a large bowl. Stir in cheese, bell peppers, zucchini, mushrooms, pasta sauce and oregano.
3. Spray a baking dish with nonstick cooking spray. Spoon pasta mixture into dish. Sprinkle it with the remaining cheese.
4. Bake for 20 to 25 minutes or until heated through and the cheese is melted.
5. Remove from the oven and let it stand 5 minutes before serving.

Vegetarian

MOROCCAN ROOT VEGETABLE TAGINE

Time: 30 mins | Serves 4
Net carbs: 38g | Fat: 4g
Protein: 7g | Kcal: 212

INGREDIENTS

- 1 tbsp virgin olive oil
- 1 red onion, chopped
- 800 g / 28 oz whole peeled tomatoes
- 450 g / 1 lb sweet potatoes, chopped
- 450 g / 1 lb parsnips, chopped
- 225 g / ½ lb turnips, chopped
- 55 g / 2 oz golden raisins
- Salt
- Freshly ground black pepper
- 125 g / 4 ½ oz fat-free plain Greek yogurt
- 1 tsp fresh lemon juice
- 60 g / 2 oz loosely packed parsley leaves, chopped

INSTRUCTIONS

1. In a Dutch pot or large heavy-bottom stockpot over medium heat, add the oil and heat until shimmering. Add the onion; cook, stirring often, 3 minutes or until the onion is softened.
2. Gently crush the tomatoes with your hands and add to the pot with the onions. Add the sweet potatoes, parsnips, turnips, raisins and 430 ml / 15 oz water. Season with salt and pepper; cook, until boiling. Reduce heat to medium and simmer, stirring occasionally, 20 minutes or until the vegetables are tender.
3. Meanwhile, in a medium bowl, combine the yogurt and lemon juice. Season to taste with salt and pepper. Set aside.
4. Transfer vegetable tagine into a serving dish. Garnish with parsley. Serve with yogurt mixture on the side.

TURKISH STUFFED EGGPLANT

Time: 3 hrs 30 mins | Serves 4
Net carbs: 41g | Fat: 24g
Protein: 11g | Kcal: 404

INGREDIENTS

- 4 small eggplants, halved lengthwise
- 70 ml / 2 ½ oz olive oil
- 1 medium onion, minced
- 4 cloves garlic, minced
- 680 g / 1 ½ lb plum tomatoes, peeled and chopped
- 2 tsp sugar
- Salt
- 2 tsp minced fresh oregano leaves
- ¼ tsp ground cinnamon
- ⅛ tsp cayenne pepper
- 60 g / 2 oz Pecorino Romano, grated
- 70 g / 2 ½ oz pine nuts, toasted
- 1 tbsp red wine vinegar
- 15 g / ½ oz finely chopped fresh parsley leaves
- 2 tbsp finely chopped fresh dill
- 70 ml / 2 ½ oz water
- 2 tbsp lemon juice

INSTRUCTIONS

1. Preheat the oven to 230°C / 450°F.
2. Line a rimmed baking sheet with foil and brush with olive oil. Arrange eggplants on a baking sheet and bake for 20 minutes, or until the skin begins to shrivel. Transfer, cut-side down, to a colander set over a sink. Let stand for 30 minutes to drain.
3. Meanwhile, in a large skillet over medium heat add the oil and heat until shimmering. Add the onions and cook, stirring often, 5 minutes or until the onions are softened. Add the garlic and cook, stirring, 1 minute or until fragrant. Transfer mixture to a large bowl.
4. Stir in the tomatoes, parsley, dill, 1 tsp sugar and 1 tbsp oil. Season with salt.
5. Transfer the eggplants and cut the side up to the skillet. Season with salt. Spoon the onion-tomato mixture into each eggplant.
6. In a medium bowl, combine the remaining oil, the remaining sugar, the water and lemon juice. Drizzle mixture all over the eggplants.
7. Cover the skillet and cook over low heat for 1 to 1 ½ hours, basting occasionally with the pan juices and adding more water if needed, until the eggplants are almost flat and the juices are caramelized. Remove from heat, spoon juices over eggplant and let cool in the skillet. Serve at room temperature.

GREEK HAND PIES

Time: 1 hr 10 mins | Serves 4
Net carbs: 77g | Fat: 27g
Protein: 11g | Kcal: 609

INGREDIENTS

- 450 g / 1 lb fresh pizza dough
- 2 tbsp virgin olive oil
- 6 green onions, white and light green parts sliced
- 680 g / 1 ½ lb mixed greens, such as spinach and arugula, coarsely chopped
- 70 g / 2 ½ oz chopped dill
- 25 g / 1 oz chopped fresh oregano
- 55 g / 2 oz crumbled feta cheese
- 2 tbsp freshly grated Parmigiano-Reggiano cheese
- 1 large egg
- Salt
- Freshly ground black pepper
- All-purpose flour

INSTRUCTIONS

1. In a large skillet over medium heat, add the oil and heat until shimmering. Add the green onions and cook, stirring often, 3 minutes or until softened. Add the greens and cook, stirring, 2 minutes or until wilted. Stir in the dill and oregano; cook, stirring, 1 minute. Transfer mixture to a colander and let cool. Squeeze out any excess liquid.
2. In a large bowl, lightly beat the egg. Stir in the greens, feta, Parmigiano-Reggiano, ½ tsp salt and ¼ tsp pepper.
3. Preheat the oven to 205°C / 400°F.
4. Lightly flour a large, rimmed baking sheet. Set aside.
5. Divide the dough into 4 equal pieces. Lightly flour a work surface and roll out each piece into a circle.
6. Mound one-fourth of the filling on the lower half of each circle. Fold the dough over to make a half-moon; press the edge of the dough to seal. Using a lightly floured fork, crimp the edges of the dough.
7. Transfer the hand pies to the prepared baking sheet.
8. Bake for 1 hour or until the crust is golden brown and the filling is hot. Serve immediately.

CHICKPEA, ZUCCHINI AND TOMATOES WITH PESTO

Time: 30 mins | Serves 4
Net carbs: 28g | Fat: 34g
Protein: 13g | Kcal: 439

INGREDIENTS

- 1 large zucchini, sliced
- Salt
- Freshly ground black pepper
- 90 g / 3 ¼ oz walnuts, toasted
- 45 g / 1 ½ oz lightly packed spinach
- 10 g / ¼ oz fresh basil leaves
- 2 garlic cloves, peeled
- 1 lemon
- 95 ml / 3 ⅓ oz virgin olive oil
- 255 g / 8 oz chickpeas, drained and rinsed
- 300 g / 10 ½ oz cherry tomatoes, halved

INSTRUCTIONS

1. Preheat the oven to 220°C / 425°F.
2. On a foil-lined baking sheet sprayed with nonstick cooking spray, arrange zucchini and season with salt and pepper. Roast 25 minutes, or until lightly browned and tender.
3. Meanwhile, add walnuts to a food processor or blend and pulse until walnuts are a fine meal. Do not over process.
4. Add the spinach, basil, garlic, juice and zest from a lemon, 2 ½ tbsp oil, ¼ tsp salt and ¼ tsp pepper, pulsing until the mixture is combined, scraping down the sides of the container as needed. Slowly blend in the remaining olive oil.
5. In a large bowl, add the zucchini, chickpeas and cherry tomatoes. Drizzle with pesto sauce, gently tossing to combine. Serve immediately or cover and refrigerate for up to 3 days.

GARLIC AND HERB LENTIL SALAD

Time: 35 mins | Serves 3
Net carbs: 49g | Fat: 19g
Protein: 17g | Kcal: 417

INGREDIENTS

- 190 g / 6 ¾ oz green lentils, rinsed and picked over
- 850 ml / 30 oz water
- 70 ml / 2 ½ oz virgin olive oil, divided
- 7 cloves garlic, minced
- 2 lemons
- 1 ½ tsp ground cumin
- ¼ tsp ground allspice
- 45 g / 1 ½ oz lightly packed fresh parsley leaves, finely chopped
- 15 g / ½ oz lightly packed fresh mint leaves, finely chopped
- Salt
- Freshly ground black pepper

INSTRUCTIONS

1. In a medium saucepan over medium-high heat, add the lentils and water; heat until boiling, then reduce heat and simmer for 20 to 25 minutes or until lentils are tender. Drain. Transfer to a medium bowl.
2. Meanwhile, in a medium skillet over medium heat, add 2 tbsp oil and heat until shimmering. Add garlic and cook, stirring, 2 minutes or until garlic is fragrant.
3. Squeeze 70 ml / 2 ½ oz lemon juice into a bowl. Whisk in remaining oil, cumin and allspice. Pour into the skillet with garlic. Cook over medium heat, stirring, about 1 minute or until heated through. Pour over lentils.
4. Stir in parsley and mint. Season to taste with salt and pepper. Serve warm or at room temperature.

Desserts

BERRIES AND HONEY GINGER YOGURT

Time: 5 mins | Serves 4
Net carbs: 59g | Fat: 12g
Protein: 11g | Kcal: 375

INGREDIENTS

- 450 g / 16 oz plain Greek yogurt
- 115 g / 4 oz honey
- 1 orange, zest
- 5 pieces crystallized ginger, crushed
- 225 g / 8 oz blackberries
- 225 g / 8 oz raspberries
- 225 g / 8 oz strawberries, hulled and sliced

INSTRUCTIONS

1. In a medium bowl, combine the yogurt, 3 tbsp honey, orange zest and ginger. Let stand for 5 minutes.
2. Evenly divide the blackberries, raspberries and strawberries into 4 dessert bowls. Top each with a large dollop of the yogurt mixture.
3. Serve drizzled, to taste, with the remaining honey.

YOGURT PANNA COTTA WITH HONEY

Time: 3 hr 10 mins | Serves 6
Net carbs: 48g | Fat: 2g
Protein: 8g | Kcal: 232

INGREDIENTS

- 1 1/2 tsp unflavored gelatin
- 1 tbsp water
- 285 ml / 10 oz fat-free milk
- 70 g / 2 ½ oz granulated sugar
- 285 ml / 10 oz low-fat buttermilk
- 245 g / 8 ½ oz fat-free plain Greek yogurt
- 2 tbsp honey
- Raspberries, blackberries or grapes

INSTRUCTIONS

1. In a small bowl, mix the gelatin with the water and let it stand for 5 minutes or until softened.
2. In a small saucepan over medium heat, add the milk and heat until simmering. Add the sugar and cook, stirring, 1 minute or until the sugar is dissolved. Remove from the heat. Stir in the softened gelatin until dissolved.
3. In a medium bowl, whisk the buttermilk and the yogurt. Whisk in the milk mixture until smooth. Pour into six ramekins. Refrigerate for 3 hours or until set.
4. Drizzle Panna cottas with honey. Serve garnished with raspberries, blackberries or grapes.

DATES WITH YOGURT, CITRUS AND HONEY

Time: 5 mins | Serves 2
Net carbs: 66g | Fat: 4g
Protein: 16g | Kcal: 344

INGREDIENTS

- 245 g / 8 ½ oz plain nonfat Greek yogurt
- 2 medium oranges, peeled
- 2 tbsp honey
- 2 dates, preferably Medjool, pitted and= chopped
- 2 tbsp chopped pistachios

INSTRUCTIONS

1. Divide yogurt between 2 bowls.
2. Cut ends off of oranges. Slice the orange into circles and then cut circles in half. Arrange over yogurt.
3. Drizzle each serving with honey.
4. Serve sprinkled with dates and pistachios.

STRAWBERRY GRANITA

Time: 4 hrs | Serves 6
Net carbs: 32g | Fat: 0g
Protein: 1g | Kcal: 126

INGREDIENTS

- 285 ml / 10 oz water
- 150 g / 5 ⅓ oz granulated sugar
- 2 tbsp lemon juice
- 450 g / 1 lb hulled and sliced strawberries plus more berries for garnish, if desired
- Fresh mint leaves

INSTRUCTIONS

1. Over medium heat in a medium saucepan add the water and sugar; cook, stirring often until sugar is dissolved.
2. Add strawberries to a blender or food processor and process until smooth. Add syrup, blending until combined.
3. Pour the mixture into a metal baking pan. Freeze for about 30 minutes or until icy around the edges.
4. Using a fork, stir icy parts into the center of the mixture. Return to the freezer, stirring edges into the center every 25 to 30 minutes, about 2 to 3 hours or until mixture is completely frozen.
5. Scrape granita into icy flakes. Cover tightly and freeze until ready to use.
6. To serve, scrape granita into bowls and garnish with additional berries or mint leaves.

STRAWBERRY TOPPED ALMOND CAKE

Time: 40 mins | Serves 12
Net carbs: 16g | Fat: 9g
Protein: 6g | Kcal: 165

INGREDIENTS

- 130 g / 4 ½ oz sugar divided
- 4 large eggs separated
- 1 teaspoon vanilla extract
- 190 g / 6 ¾ oz almond flour
- 1 teaspoon baking powder
- ¼ teaspoon salt
- 400 g / 14 oz sliced strawberries
- Greek yogurt (optional)

INSTRUCTIONS

1. Preheat the oven to 175°C / 350°F. Lightly grease a round pan with butter. Sprinkle 1 ½ tbsp sugar into the bottom of the pan.
2. In a large mixing bowl, whisk together the egg yolks, 50 g / 1 ¾ oz of the sugar and the vanilla until smooth.
3. Using a stand mixer, whip the egg whites until they form soft peaks. Slowly beat in the remaining 50 g / 1 ¾ oz sugar. Set aside.
4. Whisk together the almond flour, coconut flour, baking powder and salt. Combine with the egg yolk mixture, stirring until a thick dough forms. Working in 3 batches, fold in the egg whites, combining fully between each batch.
5. Pour the batter into the prepared pan. Bake for 30 to 35 minutes or until golden brown and a tester inserted into the center comes out clean.
6. Let the cake stand for 10 minutes or slightly cool. Run a knife around the edge of the cake. Let stand until cool.
7. Serve topped with strawberries and a dollop of yogurt (if using).

APPLE GRANOLA AND YOGURT MINI TRIFLE

Time: 5 mins | Serves 6
Net carbs: 30g | Fat: 17g
Protein: 11g | Kcal: 312

INGREDIENTS

- 2 tbsp chopped walnuts
- 245 g / 8 ½ oz granola or muesli
- 320 g / 11 ¼ oz Greek yogurt
- 120 g / 4 ¼ oz diced tart apples
- 1 ½ tbsp raisins

INSTRUCTIONS

1. In a skillet over medium-high heat, add the walnuts and toast, swirling, for 2 minutes or until fragrant. Set aside to cool.
2. In each trifle dish, layer granola, yogurt, apples and repeat. Top each with half of the walnuts and raisins.

JEWELED FRUIT EN PAPILLOTE

Time: 25 mins | Serves 4
Net carbs: 42g | Fat: 4g
Protein: 5g | Kcal: 215

INGREDIENTS

- 4 apricots, halved and sliced into quarters
- 1 honeydew melon, chopped into large pieces
- 1 peach, halved and sliced into quarters
- 4 cinnamon sticks
- 4 whole vanilla beans
- 4 tsp dry red wine
- 120 g / 4 ¼ oz plain Greek yogurt
- 2 tsp maple sugar

INSTRUCTIONS

1. Preheat the oven to 205°C / 400°F.
2. Cut 4 large sheets of parchment paper. Divide apricots, melon and peaches and pomegranate seeds evenly into the center of each piece of parchment paper.
3. Top each mound of fruit with a cinnamon stick, vanilla bean and 1 tsp wine.
4. Bring up opposite edges of the parchment paper and fold edges a few times to seal tightly. Fold up the remaining ends of the parchment, sealing tightly.
5. Transfer parchment packs to a baking sheet. Bake for 20 minutes or until the fruit is tender.
6. Cut open the parchment packets and transfer the fruit and any accumulated juices to serving plates. Serve garnished with yogurt and sprinkled with maple sugar.

FRUIT CUP CHIA PUDDING

Time: 30 mins | Serves 6
Net carbs: 38g | Fat: 18g
Protein: 7g | Kcal: 324

INGREDIENTS

- 1 cantaloupe, seeded and cut into 6 wedges
- 1.4 L / 50 oz water
- 110 g / 4 oz chia seeds
- 4 bananas
- 75 g / 2 ½ oz whole cashews
- 115 g / 4 oz coconut cream
- ¼ tsp pure vanilla extract
- Mint leaves

INSTRUCTIONS

1. Cut checkerboard-style slices into the bottom of each cantaloupe section, without cutting through the rind. Set aside.
2. In a large bowl, combine 1.1 L / 40 oz water and chia seeds. Let stand, stirring occasionally, 25 minutes or until thickened and smooth.
3. Using a blender, combine bananas, cashews, coconut cream and vanilla extract. Blend in water until mixture reaches 1.1 L / 40 oz and is the consistency of custard cream.
4. Transfer cantaloupe quarters onto serving plates. Spoon chia pudding, evenly divided, over the top of each. Pour the banana cream mixture over the top.
5. Serve garnished with mint leaves.

DRIED FIGS WITH RICOTTA AND WALNUTS

Time: 5 mins | Serves 4
Net carbs: 16g | Fat: 3g
Protein: 3g | Kcal: 101

INGREDIENTS

- 16 walnut halves
- 8 dried figs
- 60 g / 2 oz part-skim ricotta cheese
- 1 tbsp honey

INSTRUCTIONS

1. In a skillet over medium-high heat, add the walnuts and toast, swirling, for 2 minutes or until fragrant. Set aside to cool.
2. Cut figs in half crosswise and arrange on a serving plate, cut side up.
3. Using a spoon, make a small indentation on the cut side of each fig. Spoon about ¾ tsp ricotta cheese onto the top of each fig. Arrange walnut halves on top of each.
4. Serve drizzled with honey.

CHERRY CLAFOUTIS

Time: 50 mins | Serves 8
Net carbs: 38g | Fat: 5g
Protein: 4g | Kcal: 215

INGREDIENTS

- Butter
- 450 g / 1 ¼ lb sweet cherries, stemmed and pitted
- 3 large eggs, room temperature
- 60 g / 2 oz all-purpose flour
- 1 tsp pure vanilla extract
- 1 tsp grated lemon zest
- 150 g / 5 ⅓ oz granulated sugar
- 95 ml / 3 ⅓ oz milk

INSTRUCTIONS

1. Preheat the oven to 190°C / 375°F.
2. Liberally butter a shallow baking dish. Arrange cherries in a single layer.
3. Using a blender, mix the eggs, flour, vanilla extract, lemon zest, 100 g / 3 ½ oz sugar and milk until smooth. Pour the batter over the cherries. Sprinkle with 3 tbsp sugar.
4. Bake clafoutis 45 minutes or until the custard is set and a knife inserted in the center comes out mostly clean.
5. Serve warm, at room temperature or chilled.

TURKISH YOGURT CAKE

Time: 50 mins | Serves 8
Net carbs: 38g | Fat: 5g
Protein: 4g | Kcal: 215

INGREDIENTS

- 40 g / 1 ½ oz golden raisins, roughly chopped
- Muscat or sherry
- 5 large eggs, separated
- 65 g / 2 ⅓ oz granulated sugar
- 3 tbsp honey
- 95 g / 3 ⅓ oz white whole flour
- 490 g / 17 oz plain Greek yogurt
- 1 lemon, zest and juice of
- 1 tbsp virgin olive oil

INSTRUCTIONS

1. Preheat the oven to 175°C / 350°F.
2. Grease a springform pan.
3. In a small bowl, add the raisins and cover them with room temperature water. Let stand for 10 minutes. Drain and set aside.
4. Using a mixer, in a medium bowl, beat the egg yolks, sugar and honey until thick and creamy. Carefully add the flour, raisins, yogurt, lemon zest, lemon juice and oil, mixing on low until well combined.
5. In a separate bowl, mix the egg whites until stiff. Stir in a large spoonful of the egg white mixture into the egg yolk mixture. Gently fold in the remaining egg whites.
6. Pour the mixture into the prepared pan. Bake for 50 to 60 minutes or until the top is browned and the cake is puffed up in the center. Transfer to a wire rack and let cool.
7. When the cake starts to pull away from the sides of the pan, loosen the remaining cake with a knife and open the springform. Let stand until completely cool.
8. Cut into six wedges and serve.

BONUS: 21 Day Mediterranean Diet Weight Loss Plan

Day 1

Breakfast: Broccoli Cheddar Egg Muffins

Time: 15 mins | Serves 6
Net carbs: 4g | Fat: 10g
Protein: 17g | Kcal: 169

INGREDIENTS

- 8 eggs
- 4 egg whites
- 1/2 tbsp Dijon mustard
- Salt
- Freshly ground black pepper
- 140 g / 5 oz frozen chopped broccoli, thawed
- 210 g / 7 ½ oz reduced-fat shredded cheddar cheese
- 2 green onions, sliced
- 60 ml / 2 oz milk

INSTRUCTIONS

1. Preheat the oven to 175°C / 350°F.
2. Spray a standard muffin tin with nonstick cooking spray. Set aside.
3. In a large bowl, whisk the eggs, egg whites, mustard, 2 tsp salt and 1/2 tsp pepper. Stir in the broccoli, cheese, onions and milk. Pour the mixture into the muffin tin.
4. Bake for 12 to 14 minutes until a knife inserted in the center comes out clean and the egg is slightly puffed.

Lunch: Classic Greek Salad (See page 21)
Dinner: Mediterranean Stuffed Chicken (See page 43)

Day 2

Breakfast: Market Vegetable Quiche (See page 11)
Lunch: Roasted Apple, Fennel and Pear Salad

Time: 35 mins | Serves 4
Net carbs: 19g | Fat: 19g
Protein: 7g | Kcal: 261

INGREDIENTS

- 225 g / 1/2 lb red apples, cored and cut into wedges
- 225 g / 1/2 lb firm pears cored and cut into wedges
- 1 fennel bulb, cored and cut into wedges
- 55 ml / 2 oz grapeseed oil, divided
- Salt
- 55 g / 2 oz thinly sliced shallots
- 1 tsp grated ginger
- 2 tbsp white balsamic vinegar
- 1 tbsp pure maple syrup
- 1 lime, zest and juice
- 2 tsp finely chopped fresh parsley
- 1 tsp Dijon mustard
- 75 g / 2 ½ oz crumbled fresh goat cheese
- 50 g / 1 ¾ oz toasted chopped walnuts
- Freshly ground black pepper

INSTRUCTIONS

1. Preheat the oven to 230°C / 450°F with racks in the upper and lower third of the oven.
2. In a large bowl, combine the apples and pears with 1 tbsp of oil and ½ tsp salt. Transfer to a large rimmed heavy-duty baking sheet lined with foil. Spread fruit into a single layer.
3. In the same large bowl, combine the fennel, 1 tbsp of oil and ½ tsp salt. Transfer to another large rimmed heavy-duty baking sheet lined with foil. Spread into a single layer.
4. Roast, turning halfway through cooking and rotating the baking sheets, 20 to 25 minutes or until browned and fork-tender. Let stand for 15 minutes to cool. Transfer to a large bowl.
5. Meanwhile, in a skillet over medium heat, add the remaining oil and heat until shimmering.
6. Add the shallots and cook, stirring often, 3 minutes or until softened and lightly browned.
7. Add the ginger and cook, stirring, 30 seconds or until fragrant. Let stand for 5 minutes to cool.
8. In a small bowl, whisk the vinegar, maple syrup, lime zest and juice, parsley, mustard, ¼ tsp salt and ¼ tsp pepper. Whisk the warm oil into the vinegar mixture until emulsified. Drizzle vinaigrette over the fruit mixture. Serve sprinkled with goat cheese and walnuts.

Dinner: Lemon Garlic Baked Cod (See page 53)

Day 3

Breakfast: Scrambled Eggs with Tomato, Spinach and Ricotta (See page 12)

Lunch: Hearty Lasagna with Lentils and Zucchini (See page 59)

Dinner: Roman Chicken with Peppers

Time: 40 mins | Serves 4
Net carbs: 7g | Fat: 16g
Protein: 46g | Kcal: 401

INGREDIENTS

- 2 tbsp virgin olive oil
- 8 skinless boneless chicken thighs
- Salt
- Freshly ground black pepper
- 1 yellow bell pepper, cut into slices
- 2 cloves garlic, minced
- 1 tbsp chopped thyme
- 1 tbsp chopped oregano
- 285 ml / 10 oz dry white wine
- 425 g / 15 oz diced tomatoes
- 140 ml / 5 oz chicken broth
- 2 tbsp capers
- 30 g / 1 oz chopped parsley

INSTRUCTIONS

1. In a large skillet over medium-high heat add the oil and heat until shimmering. Season chicken with salt and pepper. Working in batches, cook the thighs, turning once, 6 minutes or until browned all over. Transfer to a plate and repeat with remaining thighs, adding more oil as necessary.
2. Reduce heat to medium. Add the peppers and cook, stirring often, 5 minutes or until tender. Add the garlic and cook, stirring, 1 minute or until fragrant.
3. Stir in the thyme, oregano and wine; cook, scraping up any browned bits from the bottom of the skillet, 5 minutes.
4. Stir in the tomatoes and broth. Return the chicken to the skillet. Cover and cook, 15 to 20 minutes or until an instant-read thermometer inserted into the thickest part of the thigh registers 75°C / 165°F and the juices run clear when pierced with a fork.
5. Stir in the capers and parsley. Serve immediately.

Day 4

Breakfast: Loaded Veggie Bake (See page 13)
Lunch: Moroccan Root Vegetable Tagine (See page 64)
Dinner: Date and Walnut Stuffed Chicken Breast

Time: 35 mins | Serves 2
Net carbs: 33g | Fat: 34g
Protein: 41g | Kcal: 617

INGREDIENTS

- 2 tbsp virgin olive oil
- 30 g / 1 oz chopped onion
- 60 g / 2 oz dates (preferably Medjool), pitted and chopped
- 30 g / 1 oz chopped pecans
- 1 tbsp finely chopped rosemary leaves
- 85 g / 3 oz finely shredded parmesan
- Salt
- Freshly ground pepper
- 2 boneless skinless chicken breasts
- 70 ml / 2 ½ oz dry white wine, such as Pinot Grigio

INSTRUCTIONS

1. Preheat the oven to 205°C / 400°F.
2. In a medium saucepan over medium heat, add oil and heat until shimmering. Add the onions and cook for 3 to 5 minutes or until soft.
3. Stir in the dates, pecans, rosemary and parmesan. Season with salt and pepper. Set aside.
4. Cut a slit horizontally into the thickest part of the breasts to make a pocket; do not cut completely through the breasts.
5. Spoon mixture into each of the pockets packing the filling tightly.
6. Transfer breasts to a square glass baking dish. Pour wine around the chicken. Season chicken with salt.
7. Bake for 30 minutes or until an instant-read thermometer inserted into the thickest part of the breast registers 75°C / 165°F and the chicken is no longer pink in the middle. Serve immediately.

Day 5

Breakfast: Quinoa and Feta Egg Muffins (See page 14)

Lunch: Farfalle with Tomato Avocado Sauce

Time: 15 mins | Serves 8
Net carbs: 49g | Fat: 14g
Protein: 10g | Kcal: 361

INGREDIENTS

- 450 g / 1 lb whole grain farfalle
- 4 cloves garlic
- 3 tbsp extra virgin olive oil
- 1 lemon, juice
- 2 ripe avocados, peeled and pitted
- 1 Roma tomato, chopped
- 10 g / ⅓ oz chopped fresh basil
- Salt
- Freshly ground black pepper
- Parmigiano-Reggiano cheese

INSTRUCTIONS

1. Cook farfalle according to package directions.
2. Meanwhile in a blender, combine the garlic, olive oil and lemon juice and blend until smooth. Add the avocados, tomato and basil and blend until smooth. Season with salt and pepper.
3. Drain the pasta. Transfer to serving bowls and drizzle with sauce. Serve garnished with Parmigiano-Reggiano.

Dinner: Herb Roasted Lamb Chops (See page 46)

Day 6

Breakfast: Overnight Oatmeal with Fruit and Yogurt (See page 15)

Lunch: Chicken, Feta and Kalamata Wraps

Time: 5 mins | Serves 6
Net carbs: 21g | Fat: 16g
Protein: 39g | Kcal: 373

INGREDIENTS

- 1 rotisserie chicken, shredded
- 115 g / 4 oz feta cheese, crumbled
- 75 g / 2 ½ oz roasted red peppers, coarsely chopped
- 90 g / 3 oz pitted black olives, coarsely chopped
- 2 tbsp minced shallot
- 1 tsp lemon zest
- 2 tsps lemon juice
- ½ tsp salt
- ¼ tsp freshly ground black pepper
- 125 g / 4 ½ oz plain fat-free Greek yogurt
- 4 large flour tortillas
- 115 g / 4 oz arugula

INSTRUCTIONS

1. In a large bowl, combine chicken, feta, red peppers, olives, shallot, zest, juice, salt, pepper and yogurt.
2. Arrange tortillas on work service. Divide the arugula in the middle of each tortilla. Spoon one-quarter chicken mixture on top of the arugula. Roll the tortilla up tightly, tucking in one edge as you roll.
3. Wraps can be eaten immediately or tightly covered in plastic wrap and refrigerated for up to 2 days.

Dinner: Braised Chicken Breasts with Bulgur Pilaf (See page 45)

Day 7

Breakfast: Greek-Inspired Omelet

Time: 10 mins | Serves 2
Net carbs: 5g | Fat: 27g
Protein: 18g | Kcal: 337

INGREDIENTS

- 2 large eggs
- 2 tbsp water
- Salt
- Freshly ground black pepper
- 1 tbsp butter
- 30 g / 1 oz chopped baby spinach
- 2 green onions, thinly sliced
- 3 tbsp crumbled feta cheese
- 1 tbsp chopped fresh dill
- Freshly ground pepper

INSTRUCTIONS

1. In a medium bowl, gently beat eggs, water, ¼ tsp salt and a pinch of pepper.
2. In a medium nonstick skillet over medium-high heat, add the butter and heat until melted.
3. Pour in egg mixture. Continue cooking and pushing until no visible liquid remains.
4. Arrange spinach, onions and feta on one side of the omelette. Sprinkle with dill. Using the spatula, fold the omelette in half. Slide or invert the omelette onto a serving plate.
5. Serve immediately. Season to taste with salt and pepper.

Lunch: Greek Hand Pies (See page 67)

Dinner: Paella Valenciana (See page 52)

Day 8

Breakfast: Muesli with Apples and Raisins (See page 16)

Lunch: Turkish Stuffed Eggplant (See page 65)

Dinner: Salmon with Sun-Dried Tomato Couscous

Time: 20 mins | Serves 4
Net carbs: 36g | Fat: 26g
Protein: 36g | Kcal: 524

INGREDIENTS

- 1 lemon
- 455 g / 1 ¼ lb skinless salmon, cut into 4 pieces
- 67 g / 2 ¼ oz sun-dried tomato pesto, divided
- Salt
- Freshly ground black pepper
- 2 tbsp virgin olive oil, divided
- 170 g / 6 oz couscous
- 3 green onions, sliced
- 285 ml / 10 oz low-sodium chicken broth
- 2 cloves garlic, chopped
- 2 tbsp pine nuts, toasted

INSTRUCTIONS

1. Zest lemon and reserve the zest. Cut the lemon into 8 slices. Brush 1 ½ tsp pesto on each salmon piece. Season with salt and pepper.
2. In a large skillet over medium-high heat, add 1 tbsp oil and heat until shimmering. Add couscous and onions; cook, stirring often, 2 minutes or until the couscous is lightly toasted, Stir in broth, lemon zest and garlic.
3. Arrange the salmon on top of the couscous, pressing down gently to cover the bottom and sides of the salmon. Arrange lemon slices on top of salmon.
4. Reduce heat to medium-low. Cover and cook for 12 minutes or until the salmon is opaque and flakes easily with a fork and the couscous is tender.
5. Using a spatula, transfer salmon to serving plates. Ladle couscous around salmon. Serve garnished with toasted pine nuts.

Day 9

Breakfast: Blueberry Yogurt Parfait (See page 90)

Lunch: Tuna with Farfalle and Artichokes

Time: 20 mins | Serves 4
Net carbs: 27g | Fat: 17g
Protein: 18g | Kcal: 345

INGREDIENTS

- 70 ml / 2 ½ oz virgin olive oil, divided
- 2 tsp freshly grated lemon zest
- 2 tsp chopped fresh rosemary
- 1 tsp salt
- ½ tsp freshly ground black pepper
- 170 g / 6 oz tuna steaks, cut into 2 equal pieces
- 115 g / 4 oz farfalle pasta
- 55 g / 2 oz chopped green olives
- 3 cloves garlic, minced
- 300 g / 10 ½ oz cherry tomatoes, halved
- 140 ml / 5 oz white wine
- 2 tbsp lemon juice
- 140 g / 5 oz package frozen artichoke hearts, thawed and patted dry
- Chopped fresh parsley

INSTRUCTIONS

1. In a large bowl, combine 1 tbsp oil, lemon zest, 1 tsp rosemary, ¼ tsp salt and pepper. Set aside.
2. In a large heavy-bottom skillet over medium-high heat, add 2 tsp oil and heat until shimmering. Add the tuna and cook, turning once, 6 to 8 minutes or until tuna flakes easily when tested with a fork. Transfer tuna to lemon mixture, turning to coat. When cool enough to handle, break tuna into chunks.
3. Meanwhile, cook farfalle according to package directions. Drain and set aside.
4. In a large skillet over medium heat, add the remaining oil and heat until shimmering. Stir in artichoke hearts, olives, garlic and the remaining rosemary; cook, stirring, 3 minutes or until the garlic is beginning to brown. Add tomatoes and wine; bring to a boil and cook, stirring occasionally, 3 minutes or until the tomatoes are softened and the mixture has reduced slightly.
5. Stir in the farfalle, tuna, lemon juice and the remaining salt. Cook, gently stirring, about 1 to 2 minutes or until heated through. Serve garnished with parsley.

Dinner: Sirloin Ribbons (See page 91)

Day 10

Breakfast: Grab 'N Go Fruit Smoothies (See page 18)
Lunch: Watermelon Feta and Mint Salad (See page 26)
Dinner: Chicken Artichoke and Tomato Casserole

Time: 1 hr | Serves 8
Net carbs: 13g | Fat: 26g
Protein: 32g | Kcal: 403

INGREDIENTS

- 255 g / 9 oz frozen artichoke hearts, thawed and drained
- 3 tbsp virgin olive oil
- Salt
- Freshly ground black pepper
- 8 bone-in, skin-on chicken breasts
- 1 large onion, minced
- 2 tsp minced fresh thyme leaves
- 6 garlic cloves, minced
- 425 ml / 15 oz dry white wine
- 425 ml / 15 oz orange juice
- 410 g / 14 ½ oz diced tomatoes
- 1 tbsp tomato paste
- 180 g / 6 ⅓ oz black olives, pitted and coarsely chopped
- 2 tbsp chopped fresh parsley leaves

INSTRUCTIONS

1. Preheat the oven to 230°C / 450°F.
2. In a medium bowl, add artichokes, 2 tbsp oil, ½ tsp salt and ¼ tsp pepper; toss gently to combine.
3. Spread mixture into a baking dish and roast, 20 to 25 minutes or until the edges are browned. Set aside.
4. Season chicken with salt and pepper. In a large skillet over medium-high heat add 1 tbsp oil and heat until shimmering. Working in batches, add chicken, skin-side down, and cook 8 minutes or until brown. Transfer chicken to a plate. Repeat with remaining chicken, adding more oil as necessary.
5. Adjust heat to medium, add remaining oil to the skillet and heat until shimmering. Add the
6. onion and thyme; cook, stirring often, 7 minutes or until the onion is golden. Add garlic and cook, stirring, 1 minute or fragrant.
7. Stir in the wine and juice; cook, scraping up any brown bits from the bottom of the pan and stirring, 8 minutes or until reduced by half. Add the tomatoes and tomato paste; cook, stirring often, 5 minutes or until the sauce is slightly thickened. Stir in the olives. Season to taste with salt and pepper. Add sauce to the artichokes, stirring to combine. Arrange chicken, skin side up, in the sauce in between the artichokes. Bake for 30 minutes, or until the chicken is no longer pink inside and an instant-read thermometer registers 75°C / 165°F when inserted into the thickest part of the breast. Remove from the oven and let it stand for 5 minutes.
8. Transfer chicken to serving plates. Spoon artichokes and sauce over the top. Serve garnished with parsley.

Day 11

Breakfast: Baba Ghanouj (See page 19)
Lunch: Braised Chicken Breasts with Bulgur Pilaf (See page 45)
Dinner: Steamed Mussels with Tomatoes and Olives

Time: 20 mins | Serves 4
Net carbs: 23g | Fat: 15g
Protein: 33g | Kcal: 358

INGREDIENTS

- 2 tbsp virgin olive oil
- 2 medium onions, sliced
- 4 cloves garlic, minced
- ½ tsp paprika
- Pinch cayenne pepper
- Salt
- 410 g / 14.5 oz diced tomatoes, drained
- 285 ml / 10 oz water
- 910 g / 2 ¼ lb mussels, scrubbed
- 120 g / 4 ¼ oz halved pitted green olives
- 30 g / 1 oz roughly chopped fresh parsley

INSTRUCTIONS

1. In a large Dutch pot over medium heat, add the oil and heat until shimmering. Add the
2. onions and cook, stirring often, 7 minutes or until softened and golden brown. Add the garlic and cook, stirring, 1 minute or until fragrant. Stir in the paprika, cayenne pepper, 1 ½ tsp salt, tomatoes and 285 ml / 10 oz water; cook, scraping up any browned bits from the bottom of the pot until simmering.
3. Add the mussels, olives and parsley. Cover and cook for 5 to 7 minutes or until the mussels are opened. Discard any unopened mussels.
4. Spoon into individual serving bowls. Serve immediately.

Day 12

Breakfast: Shakshuka (See page 20)

Lunch: Sweet and Tangy Cucumber Salad

Time: 35 mins | Serves 4
Net carbs: 18g | Fat: 0g
Protein: 1g | Kcal: 82

INGREDIENTS

- 4 cucumbers, peeled and thinly sliced
- 1 small onion, thinly sliced
- Salt
- 50 g / 1 ¾ oz granulated sugar
- 70 ml / 2 ½ oz white vinegar
- 70 ml / 2 ½ oz water

INSTRUCTIONS

1. In a medium bowl, add cucumbers and onions. Season generously with salt. Let stand for 30 minutes.
2. Meanwhile, in a small bowl, combine sugar, vinegar and salt, mixing well until sugar is dissolved. Refrigerate.
3. Drain liquid from cucumbers. Stir in the vinegar mixture. Refrigerate for 30 minutes or until ready to serve.

Dinner: Paella Valenciana (See page 52)

Day 13

Breakfast: Roasted Red Pepper Hummus Tostadas

Time: 10 mins | Serves 4
Net carbs: 19g | Fat: 18g
Protein: 17g | Kcal: 301

INGREDIENTS

- 4 corn tortillas
- Grapeseed oil
- 6 eggs
- 100 g / 3 ½ oz diced tomatoes, divided
- 17 g / ½ oz sliced green onions, divided
- 1/2 tsp ground cumin
- 1/2 tsp garlic powder
- 1/4 tsp Salt
- Nonstick cooking spray
- Water
- 112 g / 4 oz shredded Swiss cheese
- 112 g / 4 oz roasted red pepper hummus
- 1 avocado, peeled, pitted and sliced

INSTRUCTIONS

1. Preheat the oven to 220°C / 425°F.
2. Brush both sides of tortillas with oil and place them on a baking sheet. Bake for 8 minutes or until crisp. Set aside.
3. In a medium bowl, beat eggs. Stir in tomatoes, 3 tbsp onions, cumin, garlic powder and salt.
4. In a large skillet over medium heat, add butter and heat until melted, tilting pan to coat the bottom. Add egg mixture and cook, stirring often, 3 minutes or until eggs are set and soft.
5. Remove from heat and stir in cheese.
6. Transfer tortillas to serving plates and spread with hummus. Evenly divide egg mixture among tortillas. Sprinkle with remaining tomatoes, cheese and green onions.
7. Serve topped avocado slices.

Lunch: Chickpea, Zucchini and Tomatoes with Pesto (See page 68)

Dinner: Baked Lump Crab Cakes (See page 57)

Day 14

Breakfast: Market Vegetable Quiche (See page 11)

Lunch: Kale with Pine Nuts and Raisins (See page 29)

Dinner: Marinated Shrimp and Vegetable Kabobs

Time: 1 hr 15 mins | Serves 4
Net carbs: 20g | Fat: 42g
Protein: 19g | Kcal: 524

INGREDIENTS

- Eight bamboo skewers
- 2 lemons
- 70 ml / 2 ½ oz extra-virgin olive oil
- 70 ml / 2 ½ oz red wine vinegar
- 2 cloves garlic, minced
- 1 ½ tsp salt
- ¾ tsp freshly ground black pepper
- 450 g / 1 lb large peeled uncooked shrimp
- 24 cherry tomatoes
- 2 green bell peppers, cored and cut into 24 pieces
- 24 large onions, peeled

INSTRUCTIONS

1. Preheat the oven to 205°C / 400°F.
2. Place bamboo skewers into a tray and cover with water. Set aside.
3. Squeeze 3 tbsp lemon juice into a small bowl. Cut the remaining lemon into wedges and set aside.
4. In the small bowl with the juice, whisk in the oil, vinegar, garlic, salt and pepper.
5. In a large resealable plastic bag, add the shrimp and 285 ml / 10 oz marinade, tossing to coat. Set aside the remaining marinade. Refrigerate shrimp for 30 minutes to 1 hour, turning often.
6. Remove the shrimp from the marinade. Thread the shrimp, tomatoes, peppers and onions, alternating until each skewer is filled but with a little space between each item.
7. Spray a large rimmed baking sheet with nonstick cooking spray. Arrange the skewers on the tray and brush with the reserved marinade. Roast shrimp for 5 to 7 minutes or until shrimp are pink, firm and opaque.
8. Transfer to serving plates, removing from skewers if desired. Serve immediately.

Day 15

Breakfast: Scrambled Eggs with Tomato, Spinach and Ricotta (See page 12)

Lunch: Brussels Sprouts and Chickpea Salad (See page 30)

Dinner: Braised Shrimp, Bell Peppers and Tomatoes

Time: 30 mins | Serves 4
Net carbs: 11g | Fat: 15g
Protein: 25g | Kcal: 307

INGREDIENTS

- 450 g / 1 1/2 lb extra-large peeled and deveined shrimp
- 70 ml / 2 ½ oz extra-virgin olive oil, divided
- 2 tsp anise extract
- 5 garlic cloves, minced
- 1 tsp grated zest from 1 lemon
- Salt
- Freshly ground black pepper
- 1 small onion, diced
- 1 medium green bell pepper, stemmed, seeded, and diced
- ½ tsp red pepper flakes
- 800 g / 28 oz diced tomato, 850 ml / 30 oz juices reserved
- 70 ml / 2 ½ oz dry white wine
- 2 tbsp coarsely chopped fresh parsley leaves
- Chopped fresh basil leaves
- 2 tbsp chopped fresh dill leaves

INSTRUCTIONS

1. In a large bowl, add shrimp, 1 tbsp oil, 1 tsp anise, 1 tsp garlic, lemon zest, ¼ tsp salt and ⅛ tsp pepper tossing until well combined. Set aside.
2. In a large skillet over medium heat, add 2 tbsp oil and heat until shimmering. Add onion, bell pepper and ¼ tsp salt; cook, stirring occasionally 7 to 9 minutes or until vegetables are softened. Add remaining garlic and red pepper flakes; cook, stirring 1 minute or until fragrant. Add tomatoes and reserved juice, wine, and remaining anise; increase heat to medium-high and bring to a simmer. Reduce heat to medium and simmer, stirring occasionally, 7 to 9 minutes or until sauce is slightly thickened. Stir in parsley. Season to taste with salt and pepper.
3. Reduce heat to medium-low. Add shrimp and any accumulated juices, stirring well. Cover and cook, stirring occasionally, 7 to 9 minutes or until shrimp are pink, firm and opaque.
4. Transfer to serving bowls and drizzle with remaining olive oil. Serve garnished with basil.

Day 16

Breakfast: Loaded Veggie Bake (See page 13)

Lunch: Shepherd's Salad

Time: 35 mins | Serves 6
Net carbs: 12g | Fat: 21g
Protein: 4g | Kcal: 242

INGREDIENTS

Citrus Vinaigrette
- 1/2 small shallot, quartered
- 1 orange, zest and juice
- 1 lemon
- 2 tsp Dijon mustard
- 30 ml / 1 ¾ oz extra-virgin olive oil
- 30 ml / 1 ¾ oz avocado oil
- Freshly ground black pepper
- Salt

Salad
- 1 lb tomatoes, diced
- 3 small cucumbers, diced
- 1 green bell pepper, stemmed, seeded and diced
- 1/2 small red onion, finely chopped
- 15 g / ½ oz loosely packed chopped parsley
- 1 tbsp chopped dill
- 2 tbsp chopped mint
- 1 tsp sumac
- 120 g / 4 ¼ oz loosely packed spinach
- 115 g / 4 oz crumbled feta cheese

INSTRUCTIONS

1. Citrus Vinaigrette: In a blender, combine the shallot, orange zest, orange juice, lemon juice, mustard and Combine shallot, orange zest, orange juice, lemon juice, mustard, salt and pepper. Slowly add oils and blend until smooth.
2. Salad: In a large bowl, combine tomatoes, cucumbers, bell pepper, onion, parsley, dill, mint and sumac. Drizzle the vinaigrette over the mixture, tossing well. Refrigerate for 30 minutes.
3. Add the spinach and feta, tossing well. Season to taste with salt and pepper. Add more vinaigrette to taste. Serve salad with remaining vinaigrette in a salad dressing bottle.

Dinner: Baked Snapper with Tomatoes and Olives (See page 55)

Day 17

Breakfast: Quinoa and Feta Egg Muffins (See page 14)
Lunch: Sugar Snap Pea and Radish Salad (See page 24)
Dinner: White Kidney Bean and Fennel Salad

Time: 5 mins | Serves 2
Net carbs: 47g | Fat: 8g
Protein: 19g | Kcal: 318

INGREDIENTS

- 1 lemon
- 1 clove garlic, minced
- 3 tbsp Greek yogurt
- 1 fennel bulb, stems and roots removed
- 1 green onion, sliced
- 2 tbsp finely chopped fresh parsley leaves
- 285 ml / 10 oz water
- 440 g / 15 ½ oz white kidney beans, rinsed and drained
- Salt
- Freshly ground black pepper
- 23 g / 1 oz shaved parmesan cheese

INSTRUCTIONS

1. In a small bowl, grate the zest of the lemon and add freshly squeezed lemon juice from the lemon. Stir in the garlic and yogurt. Set aside.
2. Slice the fennel bulb in half and remove the core. Thinly slice the remaining bulb. Transfer to a large bowl.
3. Stir in the green onion, parsley, and lemon garlic mixture, adding more yogurt as necessary. Season to taste with salt and pepper.
4. Serve garnished with shaved cheese.

Day 18

Breakfast: Overnight Oatmeal with Fruit and Yogurt (See page 15)

Lunch: Garlic and Herb Lentil Salad (See page 69)

Dinner: Baked Rigatoni and Cauliflower

Time: 40 mins | Serves 8
Net carbs: 51g | Fat: 14g
Protein: 17g | Kcal: 406

INGREDIENTS

- 1 lb whole-grain rigatoni
- 1 medium cauliflower
- 70 ml / 2 ½ oz virgin olive oil, divided
- Salt
- Freshly ground black pepper
- 1 tbsp capers, coarsely chopped
- 3 cloves garlic, minced
- 3 tbsp coarsely chopped sage
- ½ tsp lemon zest
- ¼ tsp red pepper flakes
- 170 g / 6 oz grated mozzarella cheese
- 55 g / 2 oz grated Romano cheese
- 75 g / 2 ½ oz coarse dry bread crumbs
- 2 tbsp chopped flat-leaf parsley

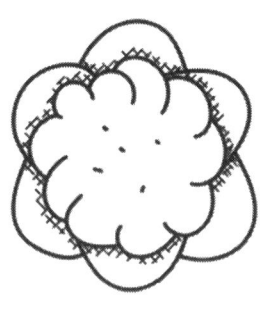

INSTRUCTIONS

1. Cook the rigatoni according to package directions to al dente. Drain. Rinse with cool water, drain and set aside.
2. Preheat the oven to 205°C / 400°F. Cut cauliflower from top to bottom and remove the core. Lay cut sides down and cut cauliflower horizontally into slices. Break into small chunks.
3. In a large skillet over medium-high heat, add 3 tbsp oil and heat until shimmering. Working in batches, arrange the cauliflower in 1 layer and cook, 2 minutes or until browned. Flip cauliflower over and cook, 2 minutes or until cauliflower is easily pierced with a fork. Transfer to a large mixing bowl and repeat with remaining cauliflower.
4. Return cauliflower to the skillet. Season with salt and pepper. Stir in capers, garlic, sage, lemon zest and pepper flakes.
5. Return cauliflower mixture to the large mixing bowl. Add rigatoni and mozzarella, tossing well. Transfer mixture to a lightly greased casserole dish. Sprinkle it with Romano cheese and bread crumbs. Drizzle with the remaining oil.
6. Bake for 20 to 30 minutes or until the top is golden and bubbly. Serve garnished with parsley.

Day 19

Breakfast: Asparagus and Mushroom Frittata
Time: 20 mins | Serves 4
Net carbs: 14g | Fat: 19g
Protein: 26g | Kcal: 326

INGREDIENTS

- 3 eggs
- 2 egg whites
- 150 g / 5 ⅓ oz parmesan cheese
- 15 g / ½ oz fresh basil leaves, torn
- Salt
- Freshly ground pepper
- 1 tbsp virgin olive oil
- 1 leek, sliced
- 450 g / 1 lb asparagus, trimmed and cut into pieces
- 225 g / 8 oz sliced baby mushrooms
- 30 g / 1 oz shredded mozzarella

INSTRUCTIONS

1. Preheat the oven to 205°C / 400°F.
2. In a large bowl, whisk eggs and egg whites. Stir in parmesan cheese and basil. Season with salt and pepper. Set aside.
3. In a large nonstick skillet over medium heat, add oil and heat until shimmering. Add leeks and cook, stirring occasionally, 3 minutes or until starting to soften. Add asparagus and mushrooms; cook, stirring occasionally, 5 to 7 minutes or until asparagus and mushrooms have softened and mushrooms have released most of their moisture.
4. Pour egg mixture into the skillet. Using a nonstick spatula, cook eggs, gently pull eggs across the pan, 2 minutes or until just beginning to set on the bottom. Sprinkle mozzarella cheese over the top.
5. Bake for 10 to 12 minutes or until the center is set.
6. Using your spatula, loosen edges and slide out onto the serving plate to serve immediately.

Lunch: Whole Grain Lasagna with Eggplant and Olives (See page 61)

Dinner: Lemon-Herb Salmon with Sicilian Caponata (See page 56)

Day 20

Breakfast: Muesli with Apples and Raisins (See page 16)

Lunch: Moroccan Root Vegetable Tagine (See page 64)

Dinner: Tuna, Green Beans and Tomatoes with Shells

Time: 15 mins | Serves 4
Net carbs: 50g | Fat: 11g
Protein: 23g | Kcal: 386

INGREDIENTS

- 225 g / 8 oz whole-grain medium pasta shells
- 225 g / 8 oz green beans, trimmed cut in half
- 2 tbsp virgin olive oil
- 2 cloves garlic, thinly sliced
- 180 g / 6 ⅓ oz cherry tomatoes, halved
- 140 g / 5 oz tuna packed in water, drained
- 90 g / 3 oz black olives, coarsely chopped
- 10 g / ⅓ oz lightly packed chopped fresh basil
- Salt
- Freshly ground black pepper
- fat-free Parmigiano-Reggiano cheese

INSTRUCTIONS

1. Cook pasta according to package directions. 2 minutes before the pasta is done, add the beans and cook until the pasta is al dente. Reserve 140 ml / 5 oz pasta water and set aside. Drain the shells and beans.
2. In a large skillet over medium heat, add the oil and heat until shimmering. Add the garlic and cook, stirring, 1 minute or until fragrant. Add the tomatoes, tuna, olives, basil and pasta water, stirring and flaking tuna with a fork, until combined. Add pasta and beans, stirring well. Season to taste with salt and pepper.
3. Transfer pasta mixture to serving bowls. Serve garnished with parmesan.

Day 21

Breakfast: Blueberry Yogurt Parfait (See page 17)
Lunch: Tuscan Baked Ziti (See page 63)
Dinner: Roasted Pork, Asparagus and Tomatoes

Time: 30 mins | Serves 4
Net carbs: 7g | Fat: 16g
Protein: 26g | Kcal: 274

INGREDIENTS

- 450 g / 1 lb pork tenderloin, trimmed
- 1 tsp dried marjoram
- ¼ tsp ground pepper
- 2 tbsp vegetable oil, divided
- 450 g / 1 lb fresh asparagus, trimmed and cut into pieces
- 1 large red onion, chopped
- 150 g / 5 ¼ oz halved cherry tomatoes
- Vinaigrette
- 1 large cloves garlic, minced
- 1 tsp minced fresh thyme leaves
- 2 tbsp fresh lemon juice
- ⅛ tsp salt
- 4 tsp extra virgin olive oil
- Freshly ground black pepper

INSTRUCTIONS

1. Preheat the oven to 205°C / 400°F.
2. Season pork with marjoram, pepper and ¼ tsp salt. In a large oven-proof skillet over medium-high add 1 tbsp oil and heat until shimmering. Add the pork and cook, turning often, about 5 to 7 minutes or until browned all over.
3. In a medium bowl, add the asparagus, onion and remaining oil and salt, mixing well. Arrange mixture around the pork.
4. Roast pork and vegetables, adding tomatoes halfway through, 12 minutes or until an instant-read thermometer inserted horizontally in the pork registers 70°C / 155°F for medium-rare to medium.
5. Transfer pork to a cutting board, cover with foil and let stand for 5 minutes. Stir vegetables with the juices in the skillet.
6. Vinaigrette: In a small bowl, whisk together the garlic, thyme, lemon juice and salt. Slowly whisk in the olive oil.
7. Slice pork, across the grain, into medallions. Transfer pork to serving plates. Arrange vegetables around the pork. Serve drizzled with vinaigrette. Season to taste with pepper.

Disclaimer

This book contains opinions and ideas of the author and is meant to teach the reader informative and helpful knowledge while due care should be taken by the user in the application of the information provided. The instructions and strategies are possibly not right for every reader and there is no guarantee that they work for everyone. Using this book and implementing the information/recipes therein contained is explicitly your own responsibility and risk. This work with all its contents, does not guarantee correctness, completion, quality or correctness of the provided information. Misinformation or misprints cannot be completely eliminated.

Printed in Great Britain
by Amazon

76947738R00066